COACHING JUNIOR SOCCER

Coaching Junior Soccer certainly fills a gap that has existed for years! This type of book has been in short supply—especially one of this calibre ... I thoroughly recommend this book to all coaches coaching at a junior level.

David Lee
National Staff Coach 1980–1998
NSW Director of Coaching 1989–1998

This book is clear, concise, easy-to-follow and understand, and will be a welcome resource for all junior coaches. A must for players, teachers and coaches alike.

Ian Greener, Coaching and Development Officer
Victorian Soccer Federation

There is no doubt that you will gain from the information and coaching practices in *Coaching Junior Soccer*, which will assist you in your training sessions ... and make you a better coach.

John Ward, Director of Coaching
Western Australia

The importance of laying sound coaching foundations for young players cannot be overstated. This book gives the coach sound advice on development principles in an easy to follow and well laid out format.

Peter Kelly, Coaching and Development Manager
Queensland Soccer Federation

ABOUT THE AUTHOR

DENIS FORD started his soccer career in England as a part-time professional player, while at the same time following a full-time career as a physical education teacher.

He was brought to Australia in 1975 by the Australian Soccer Federation as a full-time Director of Soccer Coaching, first for Tasmania and then for Queensland. He has coached senior players at State level, National League level and State League level as well as coaching State Junior teams at National Championships.

Over the past 20 years, Denis has conducted coaching courses for coaches across Australia on behalf of State Soccer Federations and Soccer Australia. These courses have ranged from teaching professional players the art of coaching at senior level, to teaching parents how to organise young children.

His qualifications include the prestigious English Football Association Senior Coaching Award, a postgraduate teaching diploma in physical education and a Master's degree in the theory of coaching. Denis is currently conducting coaching courses on behalf of Soccer New South Wales.

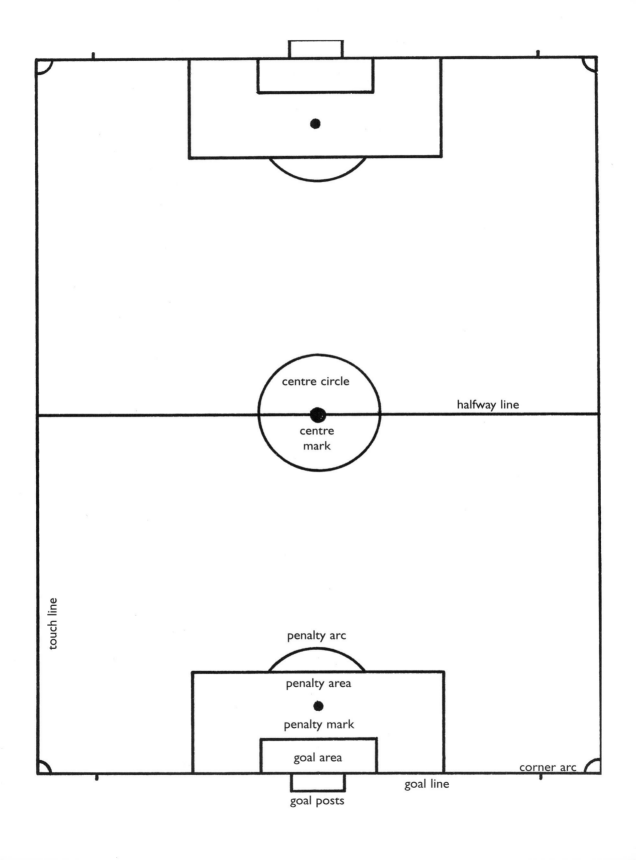

Coaching Junior Soccer

DENIS FORD

Kangaroo Press

Dedicated to my wife Kerri, our children,
and my wonderful parents

Note: In the interests of brevity, players have been referred to in the masculine. Soccer is a great game for both boys and girls, and the author strongly encourages girls to give the game a go and encourages women to become involved in the game at a coaching level.

COACHING JUNIOR SOCCER

First published in 1999 by Kangaroo Press
an imprint of Simon & Schuster Australia Pty Ltd
20 Barcoo Street, East Roseville NSW 2069

A Viacom Company
Sydney New York London Toronto Tokyo Singapore

National Library of Australia
Cataloguing-in-Publication data

Ford, Denis.
 Coaching junior soccer

 Includes index.
 ISBN 0 86417 925 1.

 1. Soccer for children—Coaching. I. Title.

796.334077

Typset in 10.5/13 pt Sabon
Printed in Singapore by Southwind Productions Pte Ltd

Contents

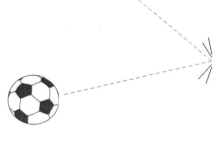

Introduction

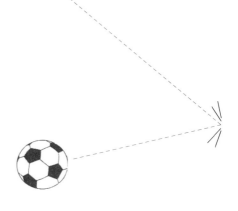

SO YOU HAVE VOLUNTEERED TO BE A COACH ...

Within Australia soccer has grown, and is continuing to grow in popularity so quickly that there are never enough experienced and qualified coaches to meet club needs. So if you are reading this book there is every likelihood that your child's soccer club were short of coaches and you have volunteered to help out.

As a volunteer it may well be that you either have no background or experience in the game, or you have played the game but have no experience as a coach. Either way you are facing a challenge for which you are probably poorly prepared. This book is aimed at providing you with that preparation. I also recommend that you attend a coaching course, details of which can be found in Appendix V.

The purpose of *Coaching Junior Soccer* is to provide coaches of six- to 12-year-olds (although 75 per cent of the information is relevant to 13-year-olds and up), with a one-stop coaching book that covers the basic requirements of being an effective junior soccer coach. This information includes:

- simple, easy to understand exercises, the majority of which are structured to enable the players to learn with little or no coaching;
- information to help you understand the varying psychological and physical needs of different age groups;
- the attributes of an effective coach and details on how to structure effective training sessions;

- guidelines on the laws of the game and dealing with injuries;
- the critical importance of coaches having the correct philosophical and attitudinal approach to coaching young children. I use the word critical because there is far too much damage being done by over-zealous coaches, parents and club officials. Having the correct philosophical approach towards young soccer players is as important, if not more important, as having first class training sessions and in-depth soccer knowledge.

Your main goal as a coach is not to win matches but to organise the children for fun and learning. Coaching has nothing to do with winning. It is to do with the development of players and helping them play well.

So please remember you are there for the kids, they aren't there for you. The kids want to enjoy themselves and winning matches is not their major goal so whatever you do, don't let your self-esteem and self-confidence be governed by whether your team wins or loses—it isn't that important!

Don't expect too much of yourself as a coach either. If you can:

- organise effective training sessions;
- help your young players improve;
- avoid turning them off the game;
- treat them fairly and decently;

then you will have done a decent job.

I hope that you find this book of assistance and use it on an on-going basis. If you have comments on this book or would like further explanations on any of the points covered herein, please write to:

Denis Ford
4 Warbroon Court
Bella Vista NSW 2153
Australia

AUTHOR'S NOTE

Age Range: Throughout the exercises I have made recommendations regarding age range. These recommendations are approximations only. For example, if you have a team of very capable eight-year-olds on your hands then they may well be able to cope with an exercise that I have recommended for nine-year-olds.

On an individual basis if you have a real talent on your hands, a soccer equivalent of a Tiger Woods, then it may be appropriate to push the player up an age group. This could well be in the interest of the team and the player. For example, if an eight-year-old playing in the Under-9 team is highly talented and way ahead of his peer group then he may dominate the game to the detriment of his team-mates, as well as not being sufficiently challenged as an individual. It may well be appropriate to move him into the Under-10 team or even the Under-11s as long as he has the mental and physical maturity to make the move.

Diagrams: These are indicative only; for example, where a team of 12 players are all performing the same exercise in pairs, one pair only may be illustrated. Player movement is indicated by a broken line; ball movement by a solid line. Where ball movement and player movement occur together (e.g. dribbling), this movement is also indicated by a solid line.

Author's Guide to Terms

The following terminology is used frequently throughout this book:

Attacking Team: When a team has possession of the ball then they are known as the attacking team. **All** the players on that team are known as attackers, even the goalkeeper. Conversely, when a team has lost possession of the ball, **all** the players are known as defenders.

Game-like Exercise: This is an exercise that focuses on a particular skill development while requiring the players to perform movements and make decisions that closely resemble real game situations.

Grid: A grid is a marked out area of the pitch in which the players perform various skills. The coach uses markers to define the area (e.g. 10 m × 15 m).

Hand Lob Serve: This is a two-handed underarm serve from one player to another.

Off the Ball: This term refers to an attacking player who does not have possession of the soccer ball.

On the Ball: This term means the player has possession of the soccer ball.

Volley: A strike performed on an airborne ball; i.e. when a player strikes a ball that is off the ground, this is known as a 'volley' or 'volleying' the ball.

In the interests of brevity players have been referred to in the masculine. Soccer is a great game for both boys and girls and the author strongly encourages girls to give the game a go and encourages women to become involved in the game at a coaching level.

SECTION I
Creating a Positive
Learning Environment

As a generalisation, if I had a choice for coach of a young children's team (say Under-6 to Under-10), between a person who really liked children but knew little about soccer, or a person who knew a lot about the game but did not really care for children, I would choose the person who liked children. (Naturally I would prefer to have someone who liked children and knew something about the game!)

The reason for this is that actual harm is being done by coaches who either become involved for the wrong reasons (such as an ambition to win premierships), or who start out with good intentions but gradually get dragged into the win-at-all-costs mentality.

It is important that any coach in charge of young children understands that successful coaching has little to do with winning or losing, but it has a lot to do with skill development as well as social and character development.

Section I will help you develop the correct philosophical approach towards coaching young children, as well as providing practical methods to maximise player learning and ensure you give the children what they want most of all—FUN!

CHAPTER 1
Your Attitude as a Coach is Critical

Coaching young children has little to do with winning. It is to do with organising them for fun and learning, helping them to develop both as players and people.

The following information is based on research with children who participate in team sports. It is straight from the horse's mouth—what the children would like to tell us. Coaches will find this knowledge invaluable for defining their approach and attitude.

A. *When asked what they enjoyed about participating in sport, children placed these statements in the following order:*
1. Improving their skill level.
2. Playing, using the skills of the sport.
3. Having a good relationship with the coach.
4. Being selected in the team, not on the bench.
5. Competing and trying to win.
6. Having an exciting, close game.
7. Being with friends.
8. Wearing the correct uniform.
9. Beating their opponents.
10. Receiving medals or trophies.

B. *In response to the prompt 'The most important thing about sport is ...', the children placed the statements below in the following order:*
1. To play as well as you are able.
2. To have fun.
3. To be fair.
4. To beat your opponent.

C. *Children feel strongly that:*
1. All players in the team should have an equal opportunity to play in matches;
2. It is more important for all players to play than for the team to win;
3. Learning to play the game is much more important than for the team to win; and
4. If they could give some advice to the coach, this is what they would say:
   - don't yell so much;
   - teach us more;
   - give us more involvement;
   - let us express ourselves;
   - don't have favourites;
   - encourage us more.

(Source: I.D. Robertson, 1987, *The Coach and the Dropout*, National Sports Research Program, Australian Sports Commission.)

The emerging theme here is that improving skill levels, being active and involved and having fun are much more important to children than winning. However, in Australian clubs there seems to be a preoccupation with winning, mainly coming from the coaches and parents, which is causing real problems with the development of young players and their retention in the sport.

Soccer is played by millions of children around the world in over 150 countries. In the majority of these countries, children play the game with a minimum of adult involvement by organising their own games in the parks, on the streets and at the beaches. They do this because soccer is a skilful and fun game to play and they love to play it!

In Australia, soccer is not seen as the

number one sport; the children don't organise themselves as much and the game has developed in a more structured manner based upon the junior club system. This has led to a high level of adult involvement, which is not always for the best as adults apply to the children an adult definition of success; that is, you are only successful as a coach if you are winning games. This adult definition of success does not match the children's definition of success, as shown by the above research. Winning games is not high on the children's lists.

There is nothing wrong with winning, but having this as the sole criteria for success in junior soccer is limiting and harmful. It also leads to some of the unsightly practices seen at children's junior soccer games at the weekend, such as hysterical and abusive sideline shouting by some coaches, parents and club officials. This results in far too much pressure being placed on the children and what should be a pleasant experience becomes an unpleasant one. The drop out rate from junior soccer is far too high and this over-emphasis on winning combined with the resultant inappropriate adult behaviours is one of the major reasons.

Adults are **turning kids off soccer** at an alarming rate, and once we realise that many coaches, club officials and parents are part of this problem, we will be able to move forward. Please remember: children are not little adults.

A NEW DEFINITION OF SUCCESS

As already stated, the problems start with the imposition of an adult definition of sporting success (i.e. winning) on children's sport, even though the children themselves place winning well down in their list of priorities.

Surely a far better definition of success for coaches, club officials and parents involved in junior soccer is: **Do all or most of the kids turn up to play next year?**

If they do turn up next year then it probably means they have:
- enjoyed the training and the games;

- are improving;
- obviously want more of the same.

It probably also means that you, the coach, have done a good job!

If they don't turn up next year then it probably means they:
- didn't enjoy the training and the games;
- haven't improved;
- don't want more of the same.

So, to ensure your kids do come back next year, read the comments from the kids at the beginning of this chapter again, and:
- make training sessions and games fun and enjoyable;
- ensure every kid is involved and active at training;
- de-emphasise winning, and focus on skill development and personal development;
- care for the kids first as human beings; and, *most importantly*
- ensure the club officials and parents are behind you in your definition of success.

Having the club and parents behind you is essential, so prior to the start of the season I suggest you take the following action:

1. Sit down with club officials and inform them that you will be focusing not on winning but on skill development, social development, and ensuring that the kids really enjoy themselves so that they develop a love for the sport and stay with the club for years to come. Make sure that the club officials are fully supportive.

2. Hold a meeting with the parents and explain that your definition of success is not winning the competition, or even winning individual games, but is for the kids to improve their skills and enjoy themselves so much that they want to come back and play again next year. Explain that winning may well be a consequence of this approach, but will not be the number one priority as it is not seen this way by the children.

At this same meeting you should detail both verbally and in the form of a handout a **Parent's Code of Behaviour** (see sample below), which will set the standards for parental behaviour for the season.

While such a code will certainly encourage correct parental behaviour, it is equally important that you, the coach, lead by example and don't do any of the things that you have asked the parents not to do. If you can do this and get the parents to understand what you are trying to achieve then everyone involved, and most of all the kids, will have an extremely enjoyable and satisfying experience.

Club Value System

As junior soccer clubs are run by adults and not by kids there is a tendency for club officials to judge the club's success in terms of the number of premierships they have won. This culture of winning filters through to the coaches and parents and starts to cause the problems of sideline shouting and inappropriate coaching behaviours and attitudes.

Children rank winning as a fairly low priority in their enjoyment of the game. It would therefore be highly productive for the club to de-emphasise winning in favour of player development and player retention and

Parent's Code of Behaviour (Sample only)

As the coach of your child my definition of success for the season is for your child to want to play again next year. This will occur, not through a focus on winning, but through:

- focusing on the child's skill development;
- ensuring the child is involved and active in all training sessions;
- adopting an approach that focuses on the child enjoying themselves.

To help me achieve the above could you please observe the following sideline rules when watching your child play at the weekend:
1. No abusive shouting
2. No destructive criticism; even collective moans and groans when a child does something wrong are very inappropriate. (How would you feel if you had a large crowd watching you play your favourite sport and they moaned every time you made a mistake?!)
3. No hysterical shouting of instructions; Calling out instructions such as 'Kick it!', 'Shoot', 'Boot it', 'Go, go, go', etc. only panics the children and is detrimental to their development as players.
4. No specific tactical instructions; Shouting out something like 'Johnny, pick up number 6', whilst it may be well-meant, only confuses the kids.

Please do not embarrass yourself, your child, or your club by engaging in any of the above behaviour. When you stop to think, it is absolutely ludicrous for a group of parents to stand on the sideline getting hysterical over a children's soccer game. Remember— to the kids this is supposed to be a day of fun and enjoyment!

By all means engage in positive, but controlled encouragement such as 'Well done, Billy', 'Great pass, Johnny' or 'Great effort, Luke'.

I look forward to providing a really enjoyable season for the children and I welcome your assistance and cooperation.

Best Regards,
Bill Smith
Coach, Bells Hills Under-9s

to establish a set of values and goals which provide direction and purpose for everyone involved in the club. (See the sample below.)

A soccer club that develops such a value system will establish a clear direction and standard of behaviour for everyone involved. Such a club will have far greater success in attracting the right type of people as coaches and managers and will develop and retain quality players for much longer.

Bells Hills Soccer Club

Our definition of success: We know we are succeeding if the children turn up to play again next year.

To achieve our definition of success the Bells Hills Soccer Club values and goals are as follows:

- to provide a positive learning environment in which children can develop their soccer skills;
- to ensure children of all abilities receive a fair go;
- to ensure the children develop a love for the game of soccer, have fun and enjoy themselves;
- to develop the social skills of the children;
- to develop the skills of our coaches on a continual basis.

We also recognise that we have an obligation to instil in our players:

- the need to respect the coach, the club and each other;
- the understanding that not everyone has the same level of ability;
- to always try their best;
- to respect the referee and the laws of the game;
- to respect the opposition and be both a gracious winner and a gracious loser.

The role of our coaches is to impart the above values and goals to the children. Their success (and our own), will be defined by the number of players who turn up to play again next year and not by the number of premierships won.

The role of club officials is to support the coaches in developing and implementing the above values and goals and to help parents achieve the values set out below:

Values for Parents

To help the club achieve the above, only positive encouragement and comment is allowed from the sideline. Please do not abuse the referee, shout at your child (including the shouting of instructions), or engage in any behaviour which is counterproductive.

The Committee
Bells Hill Soccer Club

CHAPTER 2
Qualities of a Successful Coach

The person who becomes involved with young soccer players has to become involved for the right reasons.

These should really be about enjoying the company of children and gaining enormous satisfaction from seeing them develop as players and as people; they should definitely not be connected with winning premierships.

It is so easy for the coach of young children to have their own self-esteem and self-confidence tied in with winning and losing, when being a successful coach of young children actually has little to do with the result of the game. After all, you can win as a coach simply because you have the best players. In fact, being a successful coach is much more demanding than simply winning games as it requires you to display an array of qualities and characteristics that will not only bring out the best in your players but also in you! If you have done a good job, it's not only your players who should have improved at the end of the season, but you as well!

GUIDELINES FOR AN EFFECTIVE TRAINING SESSION

One of the key qualities of a successful coach is to be able to conduct effective training sessions. By adhering to the following points, you will be well on the way to providing your players with meaningful and productive training sessions.

Rule 1: Prepare Training Sessions on Paper
Prior to a training session you should plan the structure of your session on paper, including estimated times for each activity. It is also a good idea to write down in broad terms what you want to focus on for a few months at a time, then break this down by training session.

For example, your focus for the next two months could be to have the players improve their heading skills, passing skills with the inside and outside of the foot, and their ability to create space. These broad training goals could then be developed into individual training sessions.

Rule 2: Quick Organisation
This is critical for a productive and enjoyable session and is dependent on proper planning of the training session, as outlined above. Don't have the players hanging around whilst you set things up or think of what you are going to do next. Organise and set up the next activity while the players are finishing the previous activity. Try to arrive at training before the players so you can organise the equipment and set up any areas required for small-sided games.

Rule 3: Positive and Purposeful
You need to be in charge and provide a clear sense of direction for players. This doesn't mean being overly bossy, but you should convey a positive and purposeful attitude.

Rule 4: Enthusiasm
This is of the utmost importance. You can be excused for a lot of mistakes when you are coaching, but you must be enthusiastic and

create a sense of excitement at every training session. The success of the practices you organise will depend in part on your level of enthusiasm. Players respond to an enthusiastic coach.

Rule 5: *Look and Act the Part*

To give you some immediate credibility with the players invest in a tracksuit and a pair of soccer boots. You should also avoid smoking, drinking and swearing in front of the children. Remember, you are a role model whether you like it or not.

Rule 6: *Correct Equipment*

Having the correct equipment (i.e. balls, bibs and markers) is an absolute prerequisite for an effective training session. The minimum equipment requirements for an effective coach are:

- A ball per child is essential and if the soccer club can't provide them, then insist that each child brings one to training—a reasonable ball doesn't cost that much.
- Markers (20–30 cones and/or small witches hats), are needed to mark out grids as well as pitch areas for small-sided games. Soft cones are preferable as they are easy to handle, and even if players tread on them, it is impossible for the kids to injure themselves.
- Bibs—two sets of different coloured bibs are required for team identification when playing small-sided games.

Clubs really should provide the above equipment and if they are short of funds to do so then they should dramatically reduce their expenditure on trophies—after all you can't kick a trophy!

Note: Clubs could always hand out balls at the end of season presentation rather than trophies—far more useful, as the kids can practise their skills in the off-season.

GUIDELINES FOR THE SUCCESSFUL COACH

The truly successful coach of young children:

- stays calm under pressure and doesn't yell at the children even during games;
- is well organised and looks the part;
- gets everyone involved in training and games;
- is patient, understanding and kind;
- shows lots of enthusiasm, smiles and laughs a lot;
- understands that children mature at different rates and only compares players with themselves and not with others;
- establishes standards and maintains discipline;
- praises a lot and especially praises effort;
- understands that learning should be fun— the successful coach wants the kids to enjoy themselves;

and last, but most certainly not least:

- understands that player development, not winning, is the main goal.

The successful coach has the motto *Players First, Winning Second* and understands that winning will be a consequence of player development.

The truly successful coach of young soccer players also takes a holistic approach to the development of the children and recognises that developing their soccer skills is only one part of the role of the coach. The other part involves character development, and sport presents a wonderful opportunity for the coach to instil in the players the character qualities of:

- cooperation;
- learning from mistakes;
- persistence/never giving in;
- winning and losing graciously;
- respect for opponents and officials;
- always trying their best;
- sportsmanship;
- belief in self.

One of the best ways for these characteristics to be taught is for the coach to exhibit them himself so the children can model their own behaviour on that of the coach.

The coach is a powerful role model for the kids to imitate and it most certainly should be the case of actions speaking louder than words—if the kids see the coach shake hands with the game officials and the opposing coach then they will copy this action. Through this, the children learn sportsmanship.

If the coach shows he is not going to give in when the going gets tough, then there is every chance the kids will follow his lead. Through this they will learn persistence.

If the coach is calm and composed under pressure then there is every chance that the players will also remain calm and composed under pressure.

In effect the coach is a character role model and whatever characteristics the coach displays, the kids will be bound to imitate.

The above qualities of a successful coach have little to do with technical knowledge but have everything to do with the interpersonal skills of a well-rounded person. So if you can display the above then you are well on the way to being a successful coach.

How will you know if you are successful as a coach? Well, the kids will let you know in many ways. They will:

- turn up again next year;
- ask you to coach them again next year;
- show greater enthusiasm for the game;
- demonstrate improved skills;
- accept winning and losing with grace and composure;
- turn up on time at training and not want to go home;
- give 100 per cent in games and at training.

And maybe some years down the track you will see some of your players as young adults still playing the game and thanking you for your contribution. This is probably the greatest success of all!

CHAPTER 3
How Children Learn

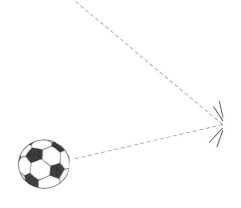

If you are involved in developing young soccer players then it is important that you understand the basic ingredients for successful learning.

The following are the six key factors in how children will learn to play soccer:
1. Repetition.
2. Fun and enjoyment.
3. Small-sided games.
4. Praise/positive reinforcement.
5. Coaching.
6. Demonstration.

These are the factors that should be present to ensure the ideal training session. However, effective training sessions can be undertaken without the two ingredients of coaching and demonstration. If you have never played the game before and/or have not attended a coaching course you can still be effective in coaching young children as long as you ensure the other four ingredients are present in your training sessions; i.e. repetition (using the appropriate exercises in this book), fun and enjoyment, small-sided games, and praise/positive reinforcement.

I. REPETITION
This is probably the main key to learning a new skill. Repetition means practising the same skill over and over again until it becomes second nature.

Taking examples from other sports, professional tennis players and golf players hit thousands of balls on a weekly basis and have a coach give them a bit of advice and feed-back so that they develop good habits. Well, the same principle applies to learning soccer—in any training session young players must have hundreds—yes, hundreds—of contacts with the ball. For young players the ball must be the centre of attention for most training sessions.

Repetition, repetition, and more repetition!

2. FUN AND ENJOYMENT
Always remember that young children play soccer for the fun of it.

It is therefore essential that the coach creates an environment and atmosphere that values fun and enjoyment. It is a myth that learning has to be a battle and a struggle. Learning is much easier and quicker if the children are enjoying themselves and let it be said that the more contacts, and preferably positive contacts a child has with the ball, the more enjoyment will result and the more learning will occur. Continuous involvement is a high priority for kids at training and the focus should be on the kids playing the game as opposed to working at it.

Obviously the coach's attitude towards the children—the way he speaks to them, the way he listens to them, the way he understands them, is very important to the creation of the right atmosphere for learning.

3. SMALL-SIDED GAMES
It is a simple fact that soccer players learn soccer by playing soccer!

New and inexperienced coaches sometimes feel they have to put on practices and coach the kids for every minute of every training session—that they must play the role of 'The Coach'. This is most definitely not the case. Small-sided games should form a substantial part of any young player's training program. In fact, they are so important that I have devoted an entire chapter to describing a variety of small-sided games for different age groups (see Chapter 4, page 21).

Small-sided games (i.e. 3 v. 3, 4 v. 4, 5 v. 5, 6 v. 6), are one of the best ways young players learn because they are much more involved and have many more contacts with the ball than in the full 11 v. 11 game. Small-sided games are an integral part of learning to play soccer and the kids love them!

4. PRAISE AND POSITIVE REINFORCEMENT
Catch the players doing something right as often as you possibly can.

Everyone loves praise and this is especially the case with young children. In fact you can ladle it on thick and fast—I doubt whether you will ever hear a child say 'I don't like my coach because he praises me too much'.

Every training session and every game is an opportunity to praise the kids, and means making a conscious decision to look for the good things the players do and praise them for doing them.

Most coaches look to catch players doing something wrong so they can put it right and there is no doubt that this is an important part of coaching. However, if you want to create a highly motivational learning environment, then you should also look for opportunities to praise as often as possible.

If you catch them doing something right and praise them for doing it, there is a strong chance that they will do it again—and isn't that exactly what you want?

After receiving such praise the child will subconsciously say, 'I liked receiving that praise, I think I'll do that action again.' So your praise will lead to the repetition of desired behaviour.

The Power of Specific Praise
Praise is much more effective if it is specific. For example, saying the following:

'Great pass Johnny, right to his feet', or 'Excellent header Johnny, right in the middle of the forehead with the eyes open' is far better than just saying 'Well done, Johnny'. Specific praise is a powerful coaching tool because it reinforces the particular action you want the player to repeat.

Praise Progress
With young players you will have to focus on catching them doing something **approximately** right, so it is important that you praise any kind of progress. You can't expect a young player to perform the skills of the game like a seasoned professional, so constantly praise them for small improvements in performing the skills of the game.

For example: 'That's a very good header Johnny, right in the middle of the forehead. Now on your next turn just make sure you keep your eyes open.'

Remember for young players learning is a long journey so don't expect perfection and ensure you praise progress along the way.

The importance of frequent praise can be best summed up by the following ratio:

I ton of specific praise to I ounce of constructive criticism

5. COACHING
You can still do a good job if you can't coach as long as you organise the kids into a productive training session.

The coaching of techniques and skills is not absolutely essential for children to learn the skills of the game. It is definitely preferable as it will speed up the learning process but it is not essential.

Obviously if you are able to coach then by all means do so, but please understand that the coaching must be of a high standard and the time spent practising skills should far outweigh the time spent coaching skills.

The ratio between practice and coaching:

I ton of practice to I ounce of coaching

Young players will learn new skills by lots of repetition. Coaching just provides them with a bit of advice to ensure they repeat the correct actions and develop good habits.

6. DEMONSTRATION
Show and Tell

If you are able to coach then a substantial part of the coaching process should be a visual demonstration of the technique to be performed. As the old saying goes, a picture paints a thousand words.

It is far better to show the skill and talk the players through it, than just to talk them through it. To the kids, this visual demonstration combined with an accompanying verbal description is just like show and tell at school. The 'show' and 'tell' work far better together than they do separately. A visual demonstration is particularly relevant to young children as they are not good listeners but are excellent imitators.

Research has shown that demonstrations should be at normal speed. It is perfectly fine to demonstrate the skill in slow motion to emphasise a point, but you should finish with a demonstration at normal speed.

So if you have the ability, show and tell on a regular basis, then let them practise many times.

The coaching sequence for the teaching of a new skill is as follows:
1. Visually demonstrate the skill and verbally explain (i.e. show and tell).*
2. Let them try the skill.
3. Observe performance.
4. Praise progress and start the sequence again if necessary.

*A word of caution: Because children are such excellent imitators do not demonstrate unless you can perform the skill reasonably well, or they will copy your bad habits. By all means use a talented player within the team to demonstrate to the other children.

Once again I emphasise that it is not essential for you to demonstrate the skills of the game to be an effective junior soccer coach. So don't be put off coaching a soccer team by your lack of skill. The correct approach to dealing with the children is more important than technical skill and knowledge.

TWO MORE TIPS FOR ENSURING A POSITIVE LEARNING ENVIRONMENT

Tip 1. Praise in Public and Criticise in Private
I don't think there will be a person reading this book who relishes the thought of being criticised in front of other people; yet we do this to our children. By all means praise in front of the other children as often as possible (and aim to share this praise around all the players), but try to criticise in private. So if you are addressing the whole group, then by all means:

■ Do say things like:
'Everybody just stop for a second and watch Johnny head the ball—look at the way he heads the ball in the middle of the forehead with his eyes open. Excellent technique, Johnny, well done.'

- **Avoid saying things like:**
  'Luke, that's not the way to do it—how many times have I told you not to use the top of the head? Now do it properly.'

Constant repetition of the first phrase will build self-confidence, self-esteem and improve skill development. Constant repetition of the second phrase will reduce self-confidence and self-esteem and won't improve skill levels as the player is not being told how to perform the skill correctly.

Coaches should therefore focus their instructions on what to do instead of what not to do.

This means you would use the coaching sequence on page 18, to assist the player who is heading the ball incorrectly. For example:

Show and tell: 'Luke, you will hurt yourself if you head the ball on top of the head. What you need to do is head the ball in the middle of the forehead like this' (visual demonstration by self or another player);

Let the player try the skill: 'Okay, now you have a go' (player has a try);

Observe performance: If he performs the skill correctly, praise him immediately—'Well done Luke, that was correct—right in the middle of the forehead'.

If he performs the skill incorrectly then *praise progress* and start the coaching sequence again: 'Luke, you have met the ball with the centre of the forehead—well done! What you need to do now is keep your eyes open as you head the ball, just like this' (visual demonstration).

When the player performs the skill correctly, reinforce the learning process with some specific praise—'Well done Luke, you headed the ball in the centre of the forehead with your eyes open. Keep on doing that, well done, excellent!'. **The player will then know exactly what he did right, so he can do it again.**

All the above correction can and should be undertaken in a quiet personal manner so the player does not feel intimidated, threatened or embarrassed. Even though you feel you have corrected the player with tact and diplomacy he may feel that just being corrected is in itself threatening. So criticise in private and praise in public.

Tip 2. It's Okay for the Kids to Make Mistakes Please let the children know that mistakes are a natural part of learning and that as long as they are trying their best it's okay to make mistakes. Explain that every time they make a mistake they should try and learn from it. In fact you may wish to substitute the phrase 'learning experience' for the word 'mistake'.

As the coach it is important to set the example in this, as nothing destroys confidence faster than focusing on the negative. This only leads to a poor learning environment for your players. The following section focuses on coaching techniques that are best avoided.

HOW CHILDREN DON'T LEARN

Far too often adults create poor learning environments for young soccer players through:

- telling the children how to perform a skill instead of showing them;
- providing little ball contact;
- over-emphasising winning;
- abusive and destructive criticism;
- hysterical sideline shouting from the coach and parents.

Just imagine how ridiculous it would be if your child attended a school where the teachers taught mathematics by:

- talking about solving a problem but never showing your child how it's done;
- only allowing your child to practise solving problems once or twice a week;
- abusing your child every time they made a mistake;
- lining the classroom with parents screaming hysterically at the kids as they worked.

You would be up in arms demanding action be taken, as you would realise that this was an appalling learning environment—yet the above happens at many soccer training sessions and at the majority of children's soccer games every week!

So, please remember that your young players will learn by lots of repetition, having fun and enjoying themselves, playing small-sided games and receiving tons of praise and positive feedback (and if you have a background in the game, by your coaching and demonstrations).

LEARNING IN THE FULL GAME

Learning also takes place in the full game the kids play at the weekend. To maximise this learning, coaches should:

- de-emphasise winning and focus on the importance of enjoying the game;
- focus on a particular skill the kids have been practising at training; for example, accurate inside of the foot passes;
- encourage interchange of positions on the field; for example, full backs overlapping, midfield players getting into shooting positions, etc.;
- rotate player positions on a weekly basis to provide the players with some experience in all positions, including goalkeeper;
- give all players at least half a game.

All of these are simple but powerful points which once implemented will complement the learning that takes place in training. To ensure there are no impediments to learning through the full game, coaches should avoid:

- screaming at the kids from the sideline;
- having the kids 'mark' a piece of the pitch waiting for the ball to come into their patch (the game just isn't played like that);
- having favourites (usually the better players), who get more of a run than the less skilled kids.

CHAPTER 4
The Importance of Small-Sided Games

The majority of professional players around the world have developed their soccer ability by playing hour after hour of small-sided games.

As children, these professional players have played either street, park or beach soccer. Without knowing it they created their own excellent learning environments through various small-sided game situations. A typical scenario probably goes something like this:

> After school a boy might decide to play by himself, kicking a ball up against a wall. A friend arrives and the two boys now play 1 v. 1. Another friend comes along and they play 1 v. 1 with a common goalkeeper. Then another friend comes along and they play 2 v. 2 with two small goals (they'll just throw their coats down for goals). As more friends turn up, they move through 3 v. 2, 3 v. 3, 4 v. 4, 5 v. 5, and so on.

They will play a variety of small-sided games for hours without parental interference or coaching. They will organise the games themselves including pitch size, rules, and even equal distribution of talent into both sides so that they have a more challenging game.

Through constant repetition and lots of ball contact in a realistic situation these young players learn ball skills, body movements, awareness, how to create space, attacking and defensive responsibilities, shooting and the crucial ability to perform in tight situations which is so essential to becoming a good player.

However, unlike some European and South American countries, soccer is not an ingrained part of Australia's culture so the kids don't get together on a regular basis for these informal games. Therefore Australian coaches need to replicate this experience by ensuring their players play lots of small-sided games at training.

This way, the kids will get lots of ball contact and repetition in game situations as well as a great deal of fun and enjoyment. If any child doesn't enjoy playing 4-, 5- or 6-a-side then they definitely should change sports!

SMALL-SIDED GAMES FOR DIFFERENT AGE GROUPS
Under Six, Seven and Eight Years

For these age groups the ideal small-sided games are 3 v. 3, 4 v. 4 and 5 v. 5. It is a fact that six-, seven- and eight-year-olds chase the ball like bees round a honey pot and as a coach there is very little you can do to change that. And why should you want to?

All these kids want to do is have fun by chasing the ball and having a kick. So you might as well go along with their natural instincts, reduce the number of kids chasing and crowding around the ball and increase their chances of getting some ball contact.

Note: Let them play at their own pace. If they go flat out for 10 minutes then slow down, that's just fine. Avoid doing any coaching when they are playing the game. Just let them play and enjoy themselves.

Suggested Pitch Size (3 v. 3 and 4 v. 4): Approximately 40 m long × 30 m wide.

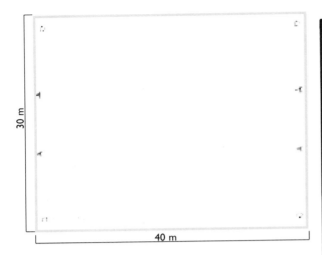

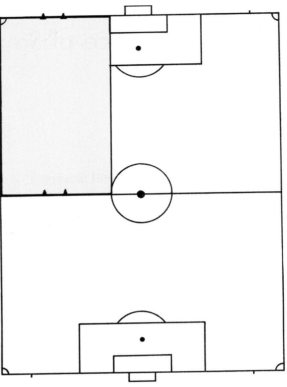

Under Nine Years and Upwards

The ideal game is 5-a-side; however, you can vary the size of the games between 3 v. 3 and 7 v. 7.

Suggested Pitch Size: A good size for a 5-a-side game is a quarter of a full size pitch.

If you are an inexperienced coach then you cannot go wrong having the players play lots of small-sided games in training. Chapter 15 (page 108) further emphasises the important role of small-sided games in the development of young soccer players. There is also a bonus—players love to play small-sided games!

Note: I also highly recommend that you allow the children to organise their own small-sided games at training. This may encourage them to do this in their own time on weekends and in school holidays.

CHAPTER 5

Maintaining Discipline

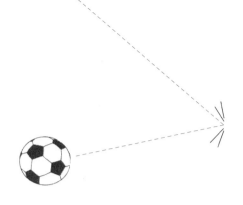

Good discipline is important for running an effective training session.

Disruptive behaviour on a regular basis at training is often due to a lack of interest on the part of the players. This is probably caused by:

- a poorly designed training session;
- the coach talking too much;
- players standing around too long between exercises or waiting for their turn;
- too much time being spent on one activity;
- implementing exercises which may be either too difficult or not challenging enough.

KEEP THE KIDS ACTIVE

The key to minimising disruptive behaviour is to ensure that all the kids are constantly involved and active in a training session and that there is a heavy focus on fun and learning.

That is why lots of ball contact and small-sided games are so important. Kids are full of energy. Their natural instinct is to want to run and play. They don't want to sit and listen to a coach talking for long periods and they don't want to be standing around doing nothing or waiting too long for their turn.

If you find that a number of players are disruptive during a practice there is every possibility that the exercise is inappropriate to their skill level, or else you have persisted with the activity for too long. This could well be the time to have a small-sided game (which, as we all know, every soccer player loves to play).

Criticise the Behaviour Not the Person

When dealing with a disruptive child never criticise the child; criticise the child's behaviour instead. For example, if the child is persistently talking while you are explaining a point:

- Avoid saying: 'Johnny you are being really disruptive, now be quiet!'

This statement is criticising Johnny as a person.

- Try: 'Johnny your talking is disrupting the group. Could you please be quiet so everyone can hear what I am saying?'

This statement is criticising Johnny's behaviour. By criticising the behaviour of the child rather than the person, you are not damaging their self-esteem and self-confidence.

LAST RESORT

If a child is constantly playing up and you have done everything possible to help correct their behaviour, you will have no option but to remove that child from the training session. This could be a temporary removal for say, 10 minutes or a permanent removal for the whole session.

If a player is persistently disruptive over a period of time, even during small-sided games, there are serious doubts as to whether that child is playing the correct sport. If this is the case it may be necessary to discuss this with the child, club officials and the parents. Removal from the team (or even the club) will have to be considered.

Note: Remember that if you are faced with disruption by a number of players, examine yourself first in respect of your training session content, levels of activity, and so on.

CHAPTER 6

Fun, Fun, and More Fun

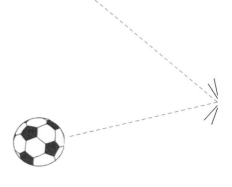

Soccer is one of the most popular junior sports in the world, played by millions of children in over 150 countries. This is because it is a fun game to play!

Unfortunately, adults have a tendency to become so emotionally involved in junior soccer that they impose their own definition of fun and enjoyment on the kids, which in many cases is based around winning. This actually turns the kids off playing the game altogether.

As a generalisation, if young children could truly articulate what fun and enjoyment meant to them, they would probably make some or all of the following statements:

Fun and enjoyment is:
1. Playing the game (not sitting on the bench for the whole game).
2. Being highly involved during training.
3. Having a supportive, positive coach who doesn't yell when I make mistakes.
4. Having a coach who recognises my efforts and improvements and praises me for trying my best.
5. Having an enthusiastic and caring coach who smiles a lot.
6. Having a mum and dad who aren't too involved (quietly encouraging me, but certainly not embarrassing me by yelling from the sideline).
7. Improving my skill level and performance.
8. Trying different positions within the team.
9. Being recognised by my team-mates as being an important part of the team.
10. Making friends and being part of the team.
11. Having exciting and close games.
12. Competing and trying to win.
13. Winning games.

Whilst the majority of the above statements will apply to children of all ages, the order of priorities will change. As children grow older their definitions of fun and enjoyment alter. Coaches need to be aware of how these definitions change as it will affect their approach to training and the game itself.

SIX- /SEVEN-YEAR-OLD CHILDREN
For six- and seven-year-olds, fun and enjoyment is simply running around like crazy trying to kick the ball and score a goal. For the majority of children at this age skill development, winning, competition tables, team focus and team spirit are not relevant.

That is why you will see little kids holding hands on the field, kicking the ball in the wrong direction and even scoring in their own goal! In fact, their definition of fun can even change with the weather so that on a rainy day all they want to do is get dirty and slide in the mud. As for winning, most kids at this age don't even know who won or lost the game and are more interested in a can of drink for afters! The score has no significance for these kids unless the parents or coach make it significant, so the coach should definitely avoid focusing on who won or lost.

Children in this age group need a totally positive approach from coaches and parents. No yelling or hysteria from the sideline, but lots of involvement and encouragement from a coach who doesn't take it seriously, but smiles a lot and creates an atmosphere of fun.

For this age group Points 1 to 6 (see page 24) would be most important for ensuring maximum fun and enjoyment.

Note: There is no problem with children playing the game from a very early age, as long as they enjoy the experience.

EIGHT- /NINE-YEAR-OLD CHILDREN

For this age group, fun and enjoyment now includes skill improvement and improved game performance. These children still need the same positive approach from the coach and parents as the six- and seven-year-olds, but will now require more emphasis on skill development. If they don't start to improve at this stage they could become frustrated.

Friendships will start to be made and peer recognition is becoming important. The opportunity to try different positions, including goalkeeper, is also an important part of their fun and enjoyment at this age.

Whilst these children now understand that they are competing and trying to win, winning is still not a main motivator for playing the game and the coach should aim to de-emphasise the significance of the score.

For this age group Points 1–12 would be most important in ensuring maximum fun and enjoyment.

10- /11- /12-YEAR-OLD CHILDREN

Like the six- to nine-year-olds, this age group still requires a supportive, positive coach and parents who can control their own sideline behaviour.

Many of these children will now have a highly developed desire to improve their skill levels and overall game performance. They will be open to instruction and constructive criticism from their coach. In fact the phrase, 'the more skilful I become and the better I play, the more fun I have' probably expresses the view of many players in this age group.

Players of this age will understand the importance of the team and start to play more for the good of the team. The concepts of team loyalty and team spirit can now be developed and team standards established. Friendship and peer recognition will become very important.

Fun now includes winning but it is not the most important part of the fun. They will still gain tremendous fun and enjoyment just from playing the game and even if they lose they will thoroughly relish a close, hard-fought match as long as they and the team played well. In fact they would much prefer close, exciting games to winning ten–nil every week, so it is important that the team is in the correct league.

Whilst winning is becoming more important the players would prefer the coach to focus on the factors that will help them win—such as effective training sessions, positive motivation, skill development, etc.—rather than having the coach stress out over the importance of winning.

All the points referred to on page 24 are still important, but there is now a greater emphasis on Point 7 and Points 9–13.

SUMMARY

Remember, for all age groups playing the game is what it's all about, and that means the game on the weekend and plenty of small-sided games at training.

Basic Skills and Exercises

The following are the techniques and exercises for the basic skills of the game. Please remember that one of the main keys to learning a new skill is **repetition**. Players must practise these skills on a constant basis in order to become competent. It is also important to give the players a chance to learn the exercise. So if you believe the activity is at the correct level, be patient, and give them the time to come to terms with it.

In my opinion there are four critical and interlinked priorities in a young player's soccer development:

- Small-sided games—See Chapter 4 (page 21) for further information.
- Awareness—Over a period of time a young player should develop the ability to be aware of what's happening around him, whilst in possession of the ball.
- Basic skills—Young players should learn the basic skills of the game through constant repetition in a variety of exercises.
- Creating space—Young players should be able to position themselves to receive the ball from a team-mate.

Many of the exercises detailed in this section are structured to ensure a *natural learning environment* where the players start to develop the correct soccer movements and skills (e.g. spreading out when a team-mate is passing the ball). The majority of the exercises require little or no coaching of the players for learning to occur. Obviously if you have played the game and have some knowledge of the game, then by all means use this knowledge to accelerate the natural learning process.

This section is focused on what the players do when they or their team is in possession of the ball. I have not included a section on defence as this can be taught at a later age and does require a degree of coaching knowledge and ability.

At the end of many of the exercises I have recommended the appropriate age range for that exercise. This recommendation is an approximation only and will vary according to the skills of your players.

CHAPTER 7

Developing Player Awareness

A player in possession of the ball must be aware of what is going on around him and the options he has available.

Awareness is an essential foundation skill of soccer. The player in possession of the ball must always be aware of where his teammates are, where the defenders are, where he is in relation to the opposition's goal, etc. To do this he must be able to get his **head up off the ball** and see as much of the field of play as possible.

If a player can get his head up off the ball then he has a far better chance of making a correct decision about what to do next. The player with the ball has a choice of five decisions to make; he can either:

- pass;
- shoot;
- dribble;
- run with the ball;
- clear the ball out of play.

In order to make one of these decisions, and preferably the correct one, a player in possession of the ball must be able to scan the field of play looking for the best option. He must be able to see his team-mates and defenders and as much of the field of play as possible.

If a player has his head down looking at the ball for too long then he'll either be unable to make a decision or he'll make it too

This player has his head up off the ball, scanning the field of play. He is therefore able to make a decision

This player has his head down looking at the ball and will probably make a poor decision as to what to do next

slowly to capitalise on a fleeting opportunity. For example, one of his team-mates may be completely in the clear, ready to receive a through ball near the opposition's goal, but if the player in possession of the ball cannot see him then he also cannot pass to him and the opportunity will be lost.

TEACH AWARENESS AT A YOUNG AGE

Developing a player's ability to get his head up and scan the field of play while in possession of the ball is virtually impossible in the early years of playing soccer. At the ages of six and seven there is little or no structure to the game and players in possession of the ball have very little opportunity to get their head up, as nearly all the players are crowded around the ball just trying to get a kick. Decision-making for the player on the ball is therefore virtually non-existent.

However, the ability to get the head up off the ball and make a correct decision is absolutely crucial later on when there is more structure to the game and team-mates are in better positions to receive a pass. It is therefore important to teach awareness as early as possible, even if the players can't use it immediately in a game situation.

If awareness is not taught at a young age, a player will have to unlearn the bad habit of always looking down at the ball and re-learn the correct habit of getting his head up and scanning the field of play, and as we all know, it is very difficult to change bad habits developed over a long period of time.

It is important that very young players learn to move with the ball while being able to see as much of the field and the other players as possible; that is, they must move with the ball with their head up, scanning the field of play.

This ability is so important that if a player can't do this well by the age of 12, then it will be an uphill task for him to become a good player.

TEACHING AWARENESS

You do not have to be a skilled coach to be able to teach awareness. All you have to do is set up the exercises outlined below and follow the subsequent instructions.

Objective: The objective in Exercises 1–8 is to teach players in possession of the ball to get their head up off the ball and be aware of what is happening around them, whilst at the same time remaining in control of the ball.

Exercise 1: Observing the Players

EXERCISE SET-UP:
- Have the players in a grid with a ball each. The size of the grid depends on the number of players. For 12 players aged 10 years, a 15 m × 10 m grid would be sufficient. Younger players would have a slightly smaller grid, older players a larger grid.
- If there are less players then mark out a smaller grid; with more players use a larger grid.

EXERCISE RULES:
Have the players move around the grid with the ball at their feet.

COACHING POINTS:
You will notice that most players have their heads down looking at the ball, which means they have little awareness of the players around them.

The following exercises will get their heads

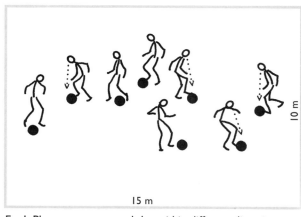

Ex. 1: Players move around the grid in different directions

up off the ball, and increase their awareness of what is happening around them.

EXERCISES TO IMPROVE AWARENESS

Exercise 2: Sole of the Foot Stop

EXERCISE SET-UP:
See diagram.

EXERCISE RULES:
Tell the players that when you raise your arm they must stop the ball with the sole of their foot.

Ex. 3: Coach simulates sitting action

Ex. 2: Coach raises arm

COACHING POINTS:
Make sure you keep walking around the grid. As you do this, don't call out—just raise your arm.
Age Range: Six–12 years.

Exercise 3: Sit on the Ball

EXERCISE SET-UP:
See diagram.

EXERCISE RULES:
The coach simulates a sitting action and the players have to sit on the ball.

COACHING POINTS:
Remember to keep walking around the grid and changing direction, so that the players have to get their heads up to look for you.
Age Range: Six–12 years.

Exercise 4: Changing Direction

EXERCISE SET-UP:
See diagram.

EXERCISE RULES:
The coach rotates an arm in the air to indicate the players have to change direction with the ball.

COACHING POINTS:
Remember to keep walking around the grid and changing direction, so that the players have to get their heads up to look for you.
Age Range: Six–12 years.

Ex. 4: Coach rotates an arm

Exercise 5: Ball Juggling

EXERCISE SET-UP:
See diagram.

EXERCISE RULES:
The coach simulates a ball juggling action with one foot, which is the signal for the players to stop and ball juggle.

COACHING POINTS:
Remember to keep walking around the grid

Ex. 5: Coach simulates a ball juggling action

and changing direction, so that the players have to get their heads up to look for you.
Age Range: Six–12 years.

Exercise 6: Dribble around the Marker
EXERCISE SET-UP:
Set up a few markers on the outside of the grid.

EXERCISE RULES:
When you make a certain signal (e.g. lift your arm horizontally), the players have to dribble the ball around the markers and back into the grid.
COACHING POINTS:
Remember to keep walking around the grid and changing direction, so that the players have to get their heads up to look for you.
Age Range: Six–12 years.

Exercise 7: Changing Balls
EXERCISE SET-UP:
See diagram.
EXERCISE RULES:
When you raise both arms in the air, each player has to stop their ball with the sole of their foot, leave that ball and dribble another player's ball.

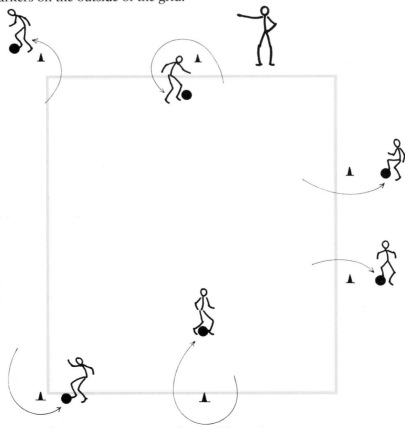

Ex. 6: Players dribble the ball around the markers

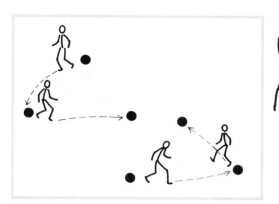

Ex. 7: Players leave their ball and move to another ball

COACHING POINTS:

Remember to keep walking around the grid and changing direction, so that the players have to get their heads up to look for you.
Age Range: Six–12 years.

Exercise 8: Touch a Player

EXERCISE SET-UP:

See diagram.

EXERCISE RULES:

As the players move around the grid with their ball, they must touch as many players as they can while retaining possession of their ball.

COACHING POINTS:

Tell the players to keep glancing up and to the side, and count the number of players touched.
Age Range: Six–12 years.

Ex. 8: Players touch as many players as possible

Exercise 9: Pass to the Coach

Objective: To encourage players to get their heads up and combine dribbling and passing.

EXERCISE SET-UP:

See diagram.

EXERCISE RULES:

- The coach calls individual players by name.
- Once called, the player must pass the ball to the coach, who passes it back to the player.
- The player returns to dribbling the ball within the grid.

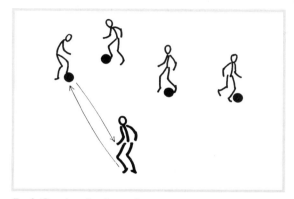

Ex. 9: Coach calls players by name

COACHING POINTS:

Remember to keep walking around the grid and changing direction, so that the players have to get their heads up to look for you.
Age Range: Six–12 years.

Exercise 10: Kick a Ball Out

Objective: To help players develop excellent head movements for watching their teammates while protecting their own ball.

EXERCISE SET-UP:

See diagram.

EXERCISE RULES:

- Tell the players to kick another player's ball out of the grid, while keeping possession of their own ball.
- When a ball is kicked out of the grid the player must immediately retrieve it and re-enter the exercise.

COACHING POINTS:

Tell the players to keep looking to the side

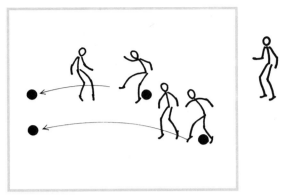

Ex. 10: Players kick as many balls as possible out of the grid

The coach indicates a stretching action, in this case for the thigh muscle

and behind them.

Age Range: Six–12 years.

You can expand on the above exercises, and as long as it achieves the objective of getting the players' heads off the ball, you'll know it's working.

OLDER PLAYERS (NINE–12 YEARS)

For older and more competent players, you could help them take their minds as well as their eyes off the ball by introducing the following progressions and variations:

(i) When the coach raises the right arm in the air, the players have to stop the ball with the sole of their right foot; if the coach raises the left arm, they must stop the ball with the sole of their left foot.

(ii) When the coach raises the right arm in the air, they must do the opposite of the above, that is, stop the ball with the sole of their left foot!

(iii) Incorporate the awareness exercises above into the warm up at the start of training. Start the warm up by letting each player dribble a ball on their own. When you make the actions for each stretching exercise, the players have to stop dribbling the ball and stretch. After each specific stretching exercise has been completed, the players continue to

dribble the ball and look for the coach's signal to perform the next stretching exercise. (For details of stretching exercises see Appendix II, page 112.)

Note: You do not have to coach for any of the above exercises—all you have to do is follow the instructions and do so in a spirit of fun.

Awareness is so important that it should be built into as many exercises as possible. There are many other practices included throughout this book which will also improve player awareness.

Remember that if a player develops the bad habit of looking down at the ball then he will never be able to play the game effectively. He must eventually have the ability, when the ball is at his feet, to get his head up off the ball and scan the field of play.

If awareness is taught at an early age and on a constant basis then it has a far greater chance of becoming a natural part of the player's technique. I would therefore suggest that some of the above exercises are used at nearly every training session for 5 to 10 minutes at a time, depending on the age group.

In addition, the coach can encourage the players to look around when they have possession of the ball during small-sided games and praise them for doing so.

CHAPTER 8

Dribbling and Running with the Ball

There is a difference between dribbling and running with the ball. However, both techniques require the player with the ball to be aware of what is happening around him.

Dribbling: The player in possession of the ball attempts to go past an opposing player or players. When dribbling in a confined space under pressure from one or more defenders, an expert dribbler glances up as often as possible in order to decide whether to pass, shoot or continue to dribble (see the diagram below).

Running with the Ball: Player runs into space with the ball, often playing the ball 1–2 m in front of himself. When running with the ball the player should be looking up most of the time, scanning the field of play so he can decide whether he is going to continue running with the ball, pass, shoot for goal, or dribble past an oncoming defender (see the diagram on page 34, top left).

DRIBBLING TECHNIQUE
The key to dribbling is to keep close control of the ball and to use body, foot and even head movements to deceive defenders. The following exercises create natural learning environments to encourage players to perform these body feints and other movements.

EXERCISES FOR DRIBBLING
Begin with the following exercises for developing dribbling ability:

This player is attempting to dribble the ball past his opponent

This player is running with the ball into space

Objective: The objective in Exercises 1–8 is to teach players dribbling skills, a feel for the ball and the ability to keep it under close control.

Exercise 1: Dribbling in the Grid

EXERCISE SET-UP:

- Have the players in a grid with a ball each.
- The size of the grid depends on the number of players; e.g. with 12 players aged 10, a grid 15 m × 10 m would be sufficient.
- If there are fewer players use a smaller size grid; for more players use a larger grid.
- Younger players would have a smaller grid, older players a larger grid.

EXERCISE RULES:

- Have the players dribble the ball around the grid.
- Encourage them to dribble the ball in different directions, keeping the ball as close to themselves as possible.

COACHING POINTS:

Once the players have got a feel for the new skill, the coach should make some of the signals from the awareness exercise every now and again, so that the players don't learn the new skill for too long with their head down.

Age Range: Six–16 years.

Ex. 1: Dribbling in the grid

Exercise 2: Changing Direction with the Ball

EXERCISE SET-UP:

See diagram.

EXERCISE RULES:

- Ask the players to first go one way with the ball, then move with the ball in the opposite direction.

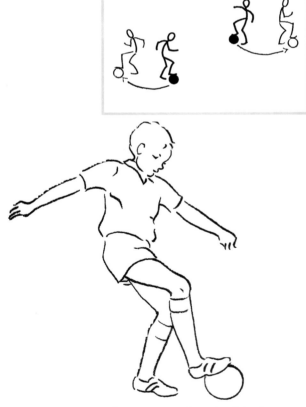

Ex. 2: Players change direction using the sole of the foot

- Get the players to try different methods of changing direction; observe the players who are performing the change of direction correctly and point out some of the different methods they use (for example, changing direction using the sole of the foot).
- Ask the individual players to demonstrate these methods to their teammates; then have everyone practise that particular method.

COACHING POINTS:
Once the players have got a feel for the new skill, the coach should make some of the signals from the awareness exercise every now and again, so that the players don't learn the new skill for too long with their head down. *Age Range*: Six–16 years.

Exercise 3: Making Shapes
EXERCISE SET-UP:
See diagram.

EXERCISE RULES:
Tell the players to make different shapes on the ground using the ball, such as a circle, square, triangle, etc.

COACHING POINTS:
Once the players have got a feel for the new skill, the coach should make some of the signals from the awareness exercise every now and again, so that the players don't learn the new skill for too long with their head down. *Age Range*: Six–16 years.

Exercise 4: Left or Right Foot Only
EXERCISE SET-UP:
See diagram.

EXERCISE RULES:
Have the players dribble the ball using their left or right foot only.

COACHING POINTS:
Once the players have got a feel for the new skill, the coach should make some of the signals from the awareness exercise every now and again, so that the players don't learn the new skill for too long with their head down. *Age Range*: Six–16 years.

Ex. 3: Players make shapes on the floor with the ball

Ex. 4: Players dribble using one foot only

Exercise 5: Tapping the Ball with One Foot

EXERCISE SET-UP:

See diagram.

EXERCISE RULES:

Tell the players to tap the ball using one foot only; first with the inside of the foot, then the outside of the foot, inside then the outside, and so on.

Ex. 6: Players tap the ball from toe to toe using the inside front of the foot

Ex. 5: Players use one foot only and tap the ball first with the inside then the outside of the foot

COACHING POINTS:

Once the players have got a feel for the new skill, the coach should make some of the signals from the awareness exercise every now and again, so that the players don't learn the new skill for too long with their head down.
Age Range: Six–16 years.

Exercise 6: Tapping the Ball Foot to Foot

EXERCISE SET-UP:

See diagram.

EXERCISE RULES:

Players use both feet to tap the ball from toe to toe using the inside front of the foot.

COACHING POINTS:

Once the players have got a feel for the new skill, the coach should make some of the

signals from the awareness exercise every now and again, so that the players don't learn the new skill for too long with their head down.
Age Range: Six–16 years.

Exercise 7A: Follow My Leader (Version 1)

EXERCISE SET-UP:

Players pair off with one ball between two.

EXERCISE RULES:

■ The player without the ball jogs around the grid weaving in and out of the other

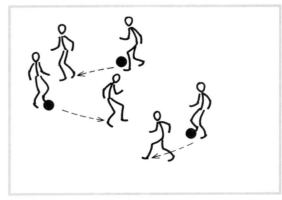

Ex. 7A: The player with the ball follows the player without the ball

players, stopping, starting, and changing direction.

- The player with the ball has to follow him.

COACHING POINTS:

Once the players have got a feel for the new skill, the coach should make some of the signals from the awareness exercise every now and again, so that the players don't learn the new skill for too long with their head down. *Age Range*: Six–16 years.

Exercise 7B: Follow My Leader (Version 2)

EXERCISE SET-UP:

Players pair off with a ball each.

EXERCISE RULES:

- One of the players with the ball moves around the grid performing changes of direction, using one foot only, tapping the ball from toe to toe, etc.
- The other player (who also has a ball) follows the first player and copies his actions.

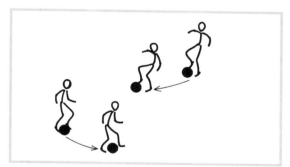

Ex. 7B: The player with a ball copies the movements of his team-mate

COACHING POINTS:

Once the players have got a feel for the new skill, the coach should make some of the signals from the awareness exercise every now and again, so that the players don't learn the new skill for too long with their head down. *Age Range*: Six–16 years.

Exercise 8: Tails

EXERCISE SET-UP:

All players tuck a training bib (tail) into the back of their shorts.

EXERCISE RULES:

- Players move around the grid with a ball at their feet and try to grab as many tails as they can. When a tail is lost, that player is out.
- The winner is the player who captures the most tails.

Ex. 8: Players try to grab the 'tails' off their team-mates

Age Range: Seven years and upwards.

Exercise 9: Ball Exchange

Objective: To combine dribbling and passing, encourage players to get their heads up off the ball and develop awareness.

EXERCISE SET-UP:

Each player has a ball.

EXERCISE RULES:

- Players dribble their ball around the grid.

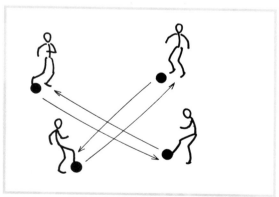

Ex. 9: Players exchange their balls with each other

- The players call to each other and exchange balls by passing to one another.

Age Range: Nine years and upwards.

INTRODUCING DEFENDERS

At some point your kids have to learn to dribble the ball past defenders as well as learn to protect the ball from the challenge of defenders. The following exercises introduce defenders into the grid to help your players learn these skills.

Exercise 10: The Coach as Defender

Objective: To encourage players to develop body feints and make them realise they have to protect the ball from defenders.

EXERCISE SET-UP:

- Have the players in a grid with a ball each.
- The size of the grid depends on the number of players; for example, with 12 players aged 10 years a grid 15 m x 10 m would be sufficient.
- If there are fewer players use a smaller size grid; for more players use a larger grid.
- Younger players would have a smaller grid, older players a larger grid.

EXERCISE RULES:

- Whilst the players are dribbling in the grid, the coach enters the grid and tries to 'win' the ball.
- This is not a serious effort to win the ball but you should make it enough of a threat for the players to react to the movements of the coach with their own unique movements.

COACHING POINTS:

- The coach should avoid using physical contact or physically intimidating the players; rather, his approach should be one of having fun by darting from player to player.

Ex. 10: The coach is in the grid 'trying' to win the ball

- Remember to keep asking the players to glance up off the ball.

Age Range: Seven/eight years and upwards.

Exercise 11: Players as Defenders

Objective: To teach players to protect the ball.

EXERCISE SET-UP:

- Grid set up as above.
- The coach sends two of the players into the grid with the instruction to win the ball from one of the other players.

EXERCISE RULES

- The defenders are only allowed to try to win the ball off a player for 5 seconds at a time. They must then move onto another player.
- The defenders may not double up on a player with the ball.
- When a defender wins possession of a ball, the dispossessed player must move to dispossess other players.

Ex. 11: Two players try to win the ball

COACHING POINTS:

Remember to keep asking the players to glance up off the ball.

Age Range: Eight/nine years and upwards.

SCREENING THE BALL

Young players have to learn how to protect the ball from the close challenge of a defender; this is known as screening the ball.

Screening Technique: The correct screening technique is for the player in possession of the ball to position his body side-on to the defender, with his shoulder leaning into the defender's chest.

The player should use the sole and outside of the foot to keep the ball away from the defender (see diagram below).

Exercise 12: Screening the Ball

Objective: For players to learn how to protect the ball.

EXERCISE SET-UP:

- The size of the grid depends on the number of players; for example, with 12 players aged ten years a grid 15 m × 10 m would be sufficient.
- If there are fewer players use a smaller size grid; for more players use a larger grid.
- Younger players would have a smaller grid, older players a larger grid.

EXERCISE RULES:

- Players pair off with a ball between two.
- Each player takes it in turn to protect the ball from their partner, who must try to gain possession.
- The coach scores the exercise by shouting out the number of seconds the attacking player retains possession of the ball from his partner.

Ex. 12: Screening—the player with the ball is side-on to the defender, with his weight on his back foot, using the outside and sole of the foot to control the ball

- Players with the ball must remain within the confines of the grid.
- Players change roles on a regular basis.

Age Range: Nine years and upwards.

OTHER DRIBBLING EXERCISES

Exercise 13: 1 v. 1

Objective: To have players practise dribbling skills with direct opposition.

EXERCISE SET-UP:

- At the ends of a grid 10 m long × 8 m wide, two cones are set up about 1 m apart for use as goals.
- Players pair off with a ball between two.

EXERCISE RULES:

- Each player attempts to score in their opponent's goals.
- Let the kids play a minute, rest a minute, play a minute, etc. During this rest they could practise individual ball juggling, or as a pair they could try keeping the ball in the air.

Ex. 13: Players play 1 v. 1

COACHING POINTS:

Tell the players to keep glancing up, looking for an opportunity to score through the goal.

Age Range: Seven/eight years and upwards.

An alternative and quick variation on the above exercise, is as follows:

Ex. 13 (variation): Players score through the other players' legs.

Players are in groups of four; two players stand 10 m distant from each other with their legs apart, while the other two players play 1 v. 1, each trying to score through their own human goal; this is done by passing the ball through one of the stationary players' legs.

Exercise 14: 2 v. 2

Objective: To have players practise a combination of dribbling and passing skills.

EXERCISE SET-UP:

■ Having set up Exercise 13, remove the markers separating the pitches so that the players now play 2 v. 2, with two goals to attack and two goals to defend.

■ You could also make the pitch size slightly longer; i.e. 15 m long × 20 m wide.

EXERCISE RULES:

Let the exercise run for about 90 seconds, followed by a rest period of 60 seconds. During the rest period the players could practise individual ball juggling or pair off and try keeping the ball in the air.

COACHING POINTS:

Tell the players to keep glancing up to look for an opportunity to score through the opponents' goal.

Age Range: Eight/nine years and upwards.

An alternative and quick variation on the above exercise is as follows:

Have four players stand with their legs apart (two at either end). The other four players play

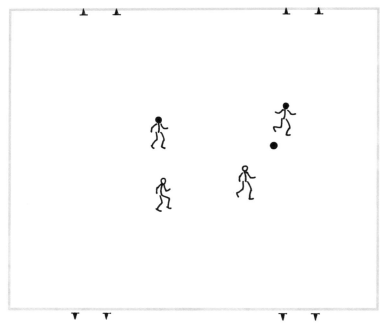

Ex. 14: Players play 2 v. 2

2 v. 2, each pair trying to score through their own human goal; this is done by passing the ball through a stationary players' legs.

Exercise 15: Dribbling to Shoot

Objective: To have players practise a combination of dribbling and shooting skills.

EXERCISE SET-UP:

- Four markers are placed about 1 m apart.
- A number of goals are set up, with a goalkeeper in each.
- Players are in groups of two or three.
- Players take it in turns to dribble the ball through the markers and shoot at the goal.

EXERCISE RULES:

Players must shoot within approximately 1 m of the last marker. This distance from goal will vary depending on the age and ability of the players. For nine-year-olds it would be about 12 m from the goal.

COACHING POINTS:

Tell the players to try and look towards the goal as much as possible whilst dribbling through the markers. Encourage them to keep glancing up with their head, not just their eyes.

Age Range: Nine years and upwards.

Exercise 16: Dribble across the Circle

Objective: To have the players develop awareness and practise dribbling the ball.

EXERCISE SET-UP:

- Players form a circle. For 12 players aged nine, the circle should be approximately 15 m across.
- Every alternate player in the circle (in this case six players) has a ball.

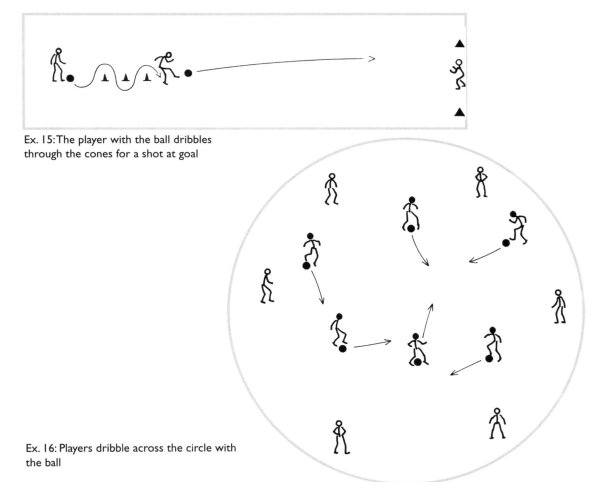

Ex. 15: The player with the ball dribbles through the cones for a shot at goal

Ex. 16: Players dribble across the circle with the ball

EXERCISE RULES:
- Each player with a ball dribbles it across the circle to a player without a ball.
- This player takes possession of the ball, then dribbles across the circle to the players without a ball and so on.

COACHING POINTS:
- Tell the players to look where they are going.
- Encourage them to get their heads up as often as possible.

Age Range: Eight/nine years and upwards.

When the players are confident with the above exercise you can introduce the following progressions:
(i)   The coach can move into the middle of the circle and feint to win the ball from the players.
(ii) Players are restricted to using one foot only.
(iii) Players must make at least one change of direction when moving across the circle.

Exercise 17: Dribble across the Square

Objective: To have the players practise close control of the ball when dribbling and to develop awareness.

EXERCISE SET-UP:
- Arrange the players in a square. For 12 players the square should be approximately 10 m × 10 m.
- The players should position themselves approximately 1 m apart.

EXERCISE RULES:
- On command from the coach the players dribble the ball to the opposite end of the square and dribble back to their original starting positions.
- The coach can repeat this three or four times.

COACHING POINTS:
Tell the players they must avoid bumping into each other and encourage them to keep glancing up.

Age Range: Seven years and upwards.

Ex. 17: Players dribble across the square

Exercise 18: Zig Zag Dribble

Objective: To have the players practise dribbling at speed and still retain control of the ball.

EXERCISE SET-UP:
- Place five cones approximately 1 m apart.
- Players are in groups of two or three.

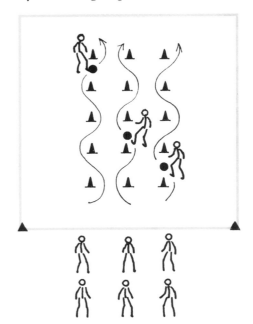

Ex. 18: Players dribble through the cones

EXERCISE RULES:

- Players take it in turns to dribble the ball in and out of the cones.
- The coach can make this into a race so that the players have to perform at speed.

COACHING POINTS:

Encourage the players to stay calm, relaxed and balanced.

Age Range: Eight years and upwards.

When the players are confident with the above exercise you can introduce the following variation:

Each player dribbles forward, stopping suddenly at each marker and starting again suddenly. Ensure that your players use the sole of the foot to stop the ball.

Exercise 19: Sole of the Foot Dribble (this consists of 3 exercises)

Objective: To develop balance and a feel for the ball.

EXERCISE SET-UP:

Players are in pairs with a ball per pair.

EXERCISE 19A RULES:

Each player hops forward on one foot and dribbles with the sole of the other foot.

Ex. 19A: Players hop forwards with the ball

EXERCISE 19B RULES:

Each player hops backward on one foot and pulls the ball with the sole of the other foot.

Ex. 19B: Players hop backwards with the ball

EXERCISE 19C RULES:

Each player moves sideways and progresses the ball by rolling the sole of the foot (furthest from the target) over the top of the ball.

Ex. 19C: Players move sideways using the sole of the foot

COACHING POINTS:

Encourage the players to think of balance and to keep glancing up off the ball.

Age Range: Seven/eight years and upwards.

Exercise 20: Dribble, Turn, Pass

Objective: To have the players practise dribbling and passing in combination.

EXERCISE SET-UP:

- Set up a series of markers about 10 m away from the players.
- Players separate into pairs.

EXERCISE RULES:

Working in their pairs, one of the players dribbles around the marker, turns, passes the ball back to his waiting partner, runs back to the starting line, and the sequence is repeated.

Ex. 20: Players dribble around their markers

COACHING POINTS:

- Encourage the players to dribble with their heads up and to always keep the ball within playing distance.
- Encourage players to try different methods of turning with the ball.

Age Range: Suitable for 8 years and upwards.

Exercise 21: Star Formation Dribble

Objective: To develop dribbling, turning and awareness skills.

EXERCISE SET-UP:

- Players are in pairs or groups of three.
- A marker is set up about 10 m away from each group of players.

EXERCISE RULES:

The first player dribbles the ball to the central marker, turns and either dribbles or passes back to the next player.

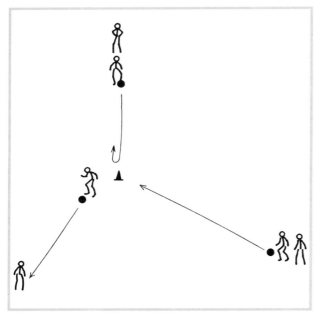

Ex. 21: Star formation dribble

COACHING POINTS:

- Encourage players to keep close control of the ball.
- Encourage players to try different methods of turning with the ball.

Age Range: Eight years and upwards.

RUNNING WITH THE BALL

The technique of running with the ball is very similar to running without the ball. Players running with the ball should use the outside front part of the foot to strike the ball in order to maintain a normal running style.

The player is running with the ball using the outside of the foot to maintain a natural running style. Notice that he has his head up scanning the field of play

EXERCISES FOR RUNNING WITH THE BALL

As we have already mentioned it is critical to scan the field of play when running with the ball. Therefore the overall objective of the following exercises is for players to improve their technique for running with the ball, and to do so with their heads up off the ball.

Exercise 22: Run towards the Coach

Objective: To have players practise running with the ball with their heads up, scanning the field of play.

EXERCISE SET-UP:

Each player has a ball.

EXERCISE RULES:

Each player runs with a ball across the pitch towards the coach, who points left or right. The players respond accordingly by moving in the direction indicated. This will ensure the players learn to run with the ball, keeping their heads up.

COACHING POINTS:

- Keep telling the players to use the outside of the foot to progress the ball.

Ex. 22: Players run with the ball in the direction indicated by the coach

- Make sure they keep looking for the coach.
Age Range: Six/seven years and upwards.

Exercise 23: Run towards Each Other

Objective: To have players practise running with the ball with their heads up, looking for and avoiding oncoming players.

EXERCISE SET-UP:

- Mark out a large grid; for 12 players the markers should define a grid approximately 15 m wide × 20 m in length.
- Players are divided into two groups with six players at either end.

EXERCISE RULES:

Two groups run at each other within the confines of a row of markers.

COACHING POINTS:

- Tell the players they must look out for each other and avoid bumping into their team-mates.
- Emphasise that all players should be using the outside of the foot to progress the ball.

Age Range: Six/seven years and upwards.

Exercise 24: Run Across

Objective: To encourage players to look sideways for players cutting across their path.

EXERCISE SET-UP:

- Mark out a grid; for 12 players define a grid approximately 20 m × 20 m.
- Divide the squad into two groups, each player with a ball.
- Each player is positioned approximately 2 m apart.

EXERCISE RULES:

Players run across the grid to the line opposite, turn with the ball and run back to their original starting point.

COACHING POINTS:

- Tell the players to avoid bumping into each other by keeping their heads up and glancing sideways.
- Remind players to use the outside of the foot to progress the ball.

Age Range: Six/seven years and upwards.

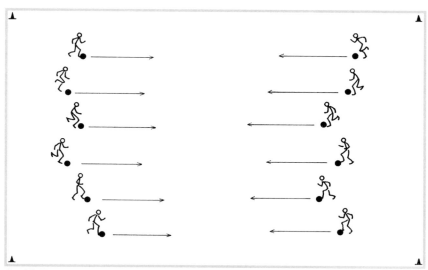

Ex. 23: Players run with the ball towards each other

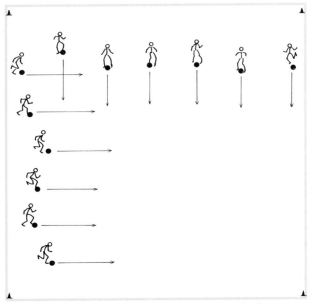

Ex. 24: Players run across the grid with the ball; reminding the players to keep their heads up

Ex. 25: British Bulldog—kids love this one!

Exercise 25: British Bulldog

Objective: To practise a combination of running with the ball and dribbling past defenders.

EXERCISE SET-UP:

- For 12 players mark out a grid approximately 20 m long × 25 m wide.
- All players (except the defender) stand approximately 2 m apart on the starting line with a ball each.
- The defender stands in the middle of grid.

EXERCISE RULES:

- The players have to run with the ball to the line 20 m away.
- The defender must try to either win the ball from one or more of the passing players, or kick it out of the grid.
- If the defender wins a ball or kicks it out of the grid, then the player who has lost possession of the ball also becomes a defender.
- The exercise continues until there are only two or three players left with a ball.
- Each time the players reach the opposite line of the grid, they must wait there until the coach tells them to run across again.

COACHING POINTS:

Players must reach the opposite line with the ball under control.

Age Range: Six/seven years and upwards.

Exercise 26: Run across the Circle

Objective: To have the players run with the ball whilst looking forwards and sideways.

EXERCISE SET-UP:

- Players form a circle large enough to ensure they can run across (approximately 25 m in diameter).
- Players space themselves approximately 3 m apart.

EXERCISE RULES:

- Every alternate player around the circle has a ball; each runs with their ball across the circle to a player without a ball.
- This player receives the ball and repeats the sequence.

Ex. 26: Run across the circle

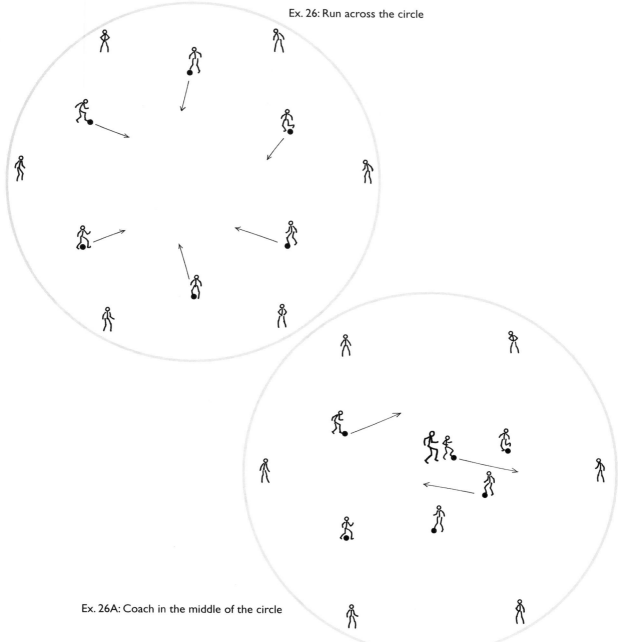

Ex. 26A: Coach in the middle of the circle

COACHING POINTS:

Tell the players to look for oncoming players as well as players cutting across from the side. *Age Range*: Seven/eight years and upwards.

As the players become competent at this exercise, the following variations can be introduced:

(i) The coach stands in the middle of the circle and 'attempts' to get the ball without any physical intimidation or tackling. This will encourage players to get their heads up to look for the coach, as well as teaching them to protect the ball. (Exercise 26A.)
Age Range: Eight years and upwards.

(ii) A couple of players can act as defenders. If one of them wins a ball, then the player who is dispossessed becomes a defender. (Exercise 26B.)

Age Range: Nine years and upwards.

(iii) When the players are approximately halfway across the circle, they call the name of a player on the outside of the circle who hasn't got a ball and pass the ball to that player. (Exercise 26C.)

Age Range: Nine years and upwards.

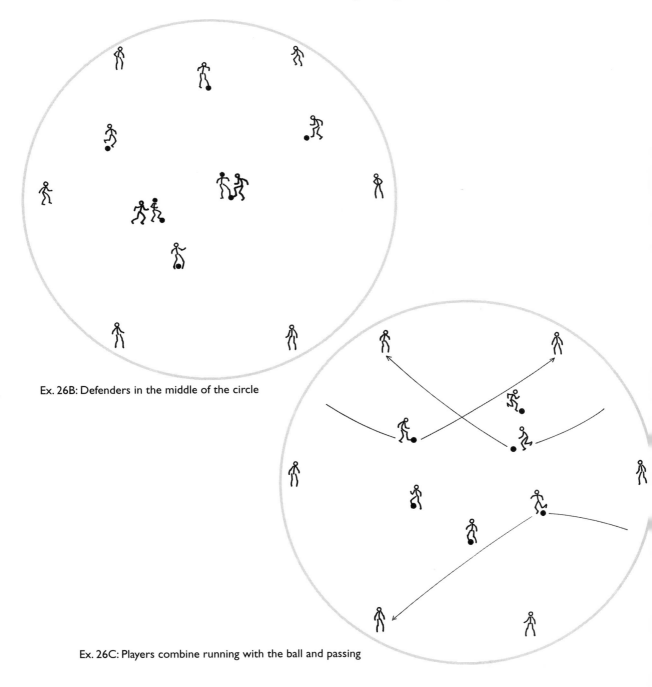

Ex. 26B: Defenders in the middle of the circle

Ex. 26C: Players combine running with the ball and passing

CHAPTER 9

Passing

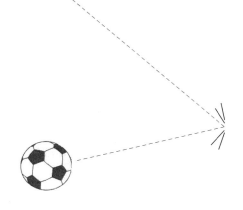

The key to learning passing techniques is plenty of repetition!

For the most part soccer is a passing game and the most frequently used passes are those played on the ground with the inside and outside of the foot.

Another commonly used pass is the long lofted pass; this is struck in the air over distance. I have not included details on long lofted passing for two main reasons:

First, young children have a real problem getting the ball in the air—they just don't have the leg strength; second, coaching the long lofted pass requires coaching expertise by an experienced coach and is not something that can be learned from a book.

This chapter therefore focuses on inside and outside of the foot passing, which young players can learn more easily.

INSIDE OF THE FOOT PASS TECHNIQUE

In classic terms the exact technique is as seen in the diagrams below. The non-kicking foot is placed alongside the ball facing the intended direction of the pass. The striking surface is the inside of the foot which is firm and 'locked' and stays in that position on the follow through.

Classic technique showing the inside of the foot pass

EXERCISES FOR INSIDE OF THE FOOT PASSING

Exercise 1: Pairs Passing

Objective: For players to practise the inside of the foot pass.

EXERCISE SET-UP:

Players get into pairs about 10 m apart with a ball between two.

EXERCISE RULES:

Each player controls the ball and passes to their partner's feet using the inside of the foot.

Ex. 1: Players in pairs using the inside of the foot pass

COACHING POINTS:

- Make sure players are on the balls of their feet and 'lively' during this exercise.
- Tell the players to follow through with the inside of their foot to the target (which in this case is their partner), as shown in the classic technique diagram, page 49.

Age Range: Seven years and upwards.

As the players improve, the following exercises can be introduced:

Exercise 2: Pass between the Markers

EXERCISE SET-UP:

- With the exact same set-up as in Exercise 1 above the coach now places two markers

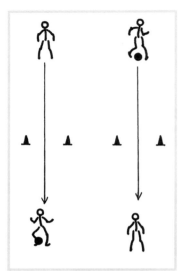

Ex. 2: Players in pairs pass between the markers

or two cones about 2 m apart at the midpoint between the two players.

- The distance between the markers can be adjusted according to the ability of the players.

EXERCISE RULES:

- The players aim to pass the ball in between the markers.
- Each player makes 10 passes with the right foot followed by 10 with the left foot.

Age Range: Seven years and upwards.

As the players become more proficient at the above exercises the following variations can be introduced (suitable for seven years and upwards):

(i) Reduce the width of the two markers from 2 m to 1 m.

(ii) Place just one marker at the midpoint between the two players and see how many times the players can hit this with an inside of the foot pass. (See Exercise 2A.)

Note: When a player knocks the marker down, his partner has to stand it back up.

(iii) Increase the passing distance between the players from 10 m to 15 m.

(iv) Practise the inside of the foot pass using

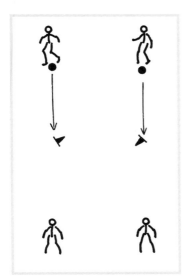

Ex. 2A: Players use the inside of the foot pass to knock the marker over

the non-preferred foot only.

(v) Have the players control the ball with one foot and pass with the other.

(vi) One-touch continuous passing. This is where two players pass the ball to each other on a continuous basis. The players would have to be very competent to perform this exercise successfully.

All of the above exercises and variations are excellent for developing the basic techniques for inside of the foot passing. However, in a game situation *defenders won't wait* while a player puts himself in the classic inside of the foot technique position.

Therefore it is absolutely essential that players practise inside of the foot passing in game-like and game situations. The following exercises allow players to develop their passing technique in more game-like situations:

GAME-LIKE PASSING EXERCISES

Exercise 3: Pairs Passing in the Grid
Objective: To practise passing and moving.
EXERCISE SET-UP:
■ Mark out a grid; for 12 players aged 10

years, this would be approximately 20 m × 20 m.
■ Players pair off with a ball between two.
EXERCISE RULES:
■ Player A passes the ball to Player B.
■ As soon as Player A has passed the ball, he must run behind one of the other players, to receive the return pass from Player B.
■ Player B then passes the ball to Player A and moves behind another player, ready to receive the return pass from Player A.
■ Players must constantly pass and move.

Ex. 3: Players pass and move

COACHING POINTS:
■ Tell the players to run away from each other; i.e. the player with the ball and his partner without the ball must run away from each other, but stay within the confines of the grid.
■ Instruct the players to keep looking for their partners, even while running away from them.
Age Range: Eight/nine years and upwards.

Exercise 4: Teams Passing in the Grid
Objective: To develop passing accuracy, player movement and support for the passer.
EXERCISE SET-UP:
■ Mark out a grid; for 12 players aged 10 years, this would be approximately 30 m × 30 m.

- Players form into teams of three or four.
- Players number themselves Player 1, Player 2, etc.

EXERCISE RULES:

- The players pass the ball in number sequence. Player 1 passes to Player 2, who passes to Player 3, who passes to Player 1 and the sequence is repeated. All teams work within the confines of the grid.
- Once a player has passed the ball, he has to run around any three players within the grid and be back in time for his turn to receive the ball again. This will ensure that the players will keep glancing at the ball while they run.

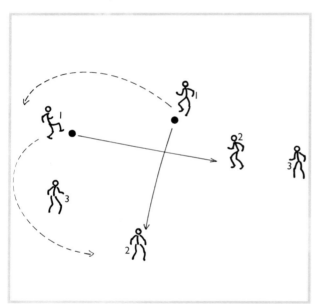

Ex. 4: Players pass the ball in sequence

COACHING POINTS:

- Tell the players to try and maintain a passing distance of at least 10 m between the player passing the ball and the receiver.
- Remind the players who are running off the ball to keep looking for the player with the ball.

Age Range: Nine/10 years and upwards.

Exercise 5: Knock the Markers Over (or Miss the Markers)

Objective: To develop accurate passing skills using the inside of the foot.

EXERCISE SET-UP:

- Mark out a circle approximately 15 m across. (This size is suitable for nine-year-olds but the circle can have a diameter of up to 20 m for older and better players.)
- A number of markers are placed in the circle.

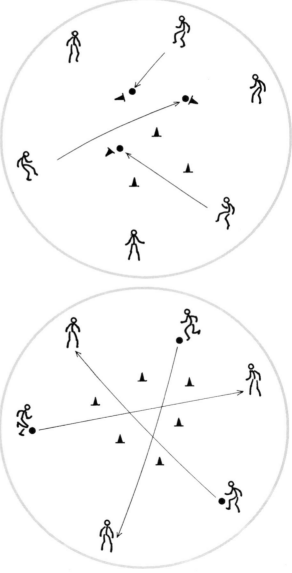

Ex. 5: Knock the markers over (or miss the markers)

EXERCISE RULES:

- The players pass the ball across the circle.
- The rules of the game can be either to knock the markers over (a point each time), or miss the markers completely (a point for every successful pass across the circle).

Age Range: Eight years and upwards.

Exercise 6: Man in the Middle Passing

Objective: To have the players practise passing and turning.

EXERCISE SET-UP:

- Three players are in a line with the middle player 10 m from each of the outside players.
- The outside players each have a ball.

EXERCISE RULES:

- The outside players take turns to play their ball to the central player.
- The middle player must control the ball, play a return pass with the inside of his foot, then turn and repeat the sequence with the other player.

Ex. 6: Man in the middle passing

COACHING POINTS:

Tell the player in the middle to stay calm but 'alive' on the balls of his feet.

Age Range: Nine/10 years and upwards.

Exercise 7: Forwards and Backwards Passing

Objective: To practise passing and moving and develop the ability to pass a ball at the correct pace.

EXERCISE SET-UP:

Players are in pairs with a ball between two.

EXERCISE RULES:

- One player moves forward while the other player moves backward, maintaining a distance of 5–10 m between them. The players pass the ball between them as they move.
- Players continue for 40–50 m, swap roles and return to the starting position.

Ex. 7: Forwards and backwards passing

COACHING POINTS:

Focus the players on accuracy and the correct pace of the pass.

Age Range: Nine/10 years of age and upwards.

Exercise 8: Pairs into Space Passing

Objective: To have the players practise passing the ball into space.

EXERCISE SET-UP:

Players are in pairs with a ball per pair.

EXERCISE RULES:

- The players move forward keeping approximately 7 m apart, passing the ball (with

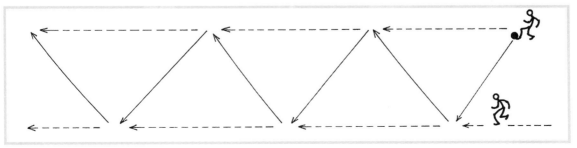

Ex.8: Pair into space passing

the inside of the foot) into the space in front of their partner.

- Players pass the ball using the foot furthest away from their partner.
- The players continue for 40 m, then return to the starting point with the players now using the other foot to pass the ball.

COACHING POINTS:
- Ensure the players pass the ball using the foot furthest away from their partner.
- The pass should arrive at the same time as the receiving player.

Age Range: Eight/nine years and upwards.

Exercise 9: File Passing

Objective: To have the players practise passing and moving.

EXERCISE SET-UP:
- Arrange players in two lines facing each other, approximately 10–12 m apart, with no more than three players in each row.
- The coach should place a marker on either side.

EXERCISE RULES:
- Players pass the ball to the opposite player, and join the back of the receiver's queue.
- The players run around the markers keeping out of the line of the oncoming pass.

COACHING POINTS:
Tell the players to control the ball to the side.
Age Range: Nine/10 years and upwards.

Exercise 10: Cross File Passing

Objective: Players will now learn when to pass the ball as well as further develop accuracy in passing by performing the action in a more game-like set-up.

EXERCISE SET-UP:
As above, players still operate in two files approximately 10–12 m apart, but now work across each other, as shown in the diagram on page 55.

This exercise is a more game-like extension of the above exercise because the players are required to make decisions about when to pass. The coach can further emphasise this by giving two instructions to the players.

EXERCISE RULES:
- If you hit another player with your pass you have to do two sit-ups.
- If you get hit with a ball whilst running through you have to do two sit-ups.

Age Range: Nine/10 years and upwards.

The above rules will encourage players with the ball to deliver the pass at the right time (which they have to do in a game), as well as encouraging the players running through to look around and be aware (which they also have to do in a game).

Note: The sit-ups should be seen as fun and not as a punishment.

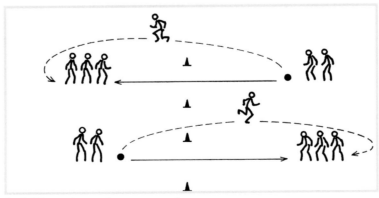

Ex. 9: File passing— players pass and move

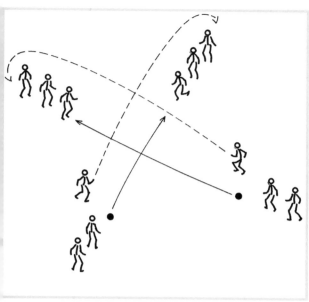

Ex. 10: Cross file passing

Exercise 11: Pass Across the Circle
Objective: This helps players practise accuracy in passing.
EXERCISE SET-UP:
- Players form a circle about 15–20 m across.
- Every alternate player in the circle has a ball.

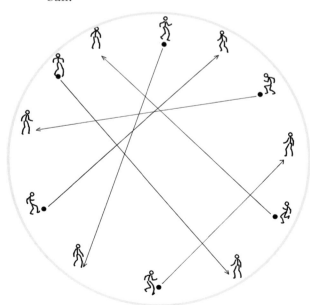

Ex. 11: Pass across the circle

EXERCISE RULES:
- Players with a ball pass it across the circle to players who haven't got a ball.
- Players in possession of a ball must call the name of the player to whom they are about to pass.

COACHING POINT:
The ball is now being passed over a longer distance; this requires the passer to focus on accuracy and power.
Age Range: Nine/10 years and upwards.

The following advanced exercises combine dribbling and passing using the inside and the outside of the foot:

Exercise 12: 2 Attackers v. 1 Defender
Objective: To combine dribbling and passing skills.
EXERCISE SET-UP:
- Play takes place in a marked out grid 20 m long × 10 m wide.
- Players are in groups of three with one ball.
- Two of the players are attackers and one player is a defender.

EXERCISE RULES:
- The two attackers have to get the ball past the defender by dribbling and/or passing; a point is scored when one of the attackers gets the ball past the defender.
- The defender scores a point by winning possession or knocking the ball out of the grid.
- Players have three turns each then change.

COACHING POINT:
The player with the ball should run at the defender and either pass to his team-mate or dribble past the defender.
Age Range: Nine/10 years and upwards.

Exercise 13: Wall Passing
Objective: To have the players combine dribbling and passing.
EXERCISE SET-UP:
- Play takes place in a marked out grid 20 m long × 10 m wide.

Ex. 12: 2 attackers v. 1 defender

- Players are in groups of four with one ball.
- Two players play 1 v. 1 with the other two players stood at the midpoint on either side of the grid.

EXERCISE RULES:
- The player in possession of the ball can pass the ball to either of the two outside players who must make a first time (one-touch) pass back to the same player.
- Every time the player with the ball gets past his opponent while keeping possession of the ball, he scores a point.
- Players change roles every minute.

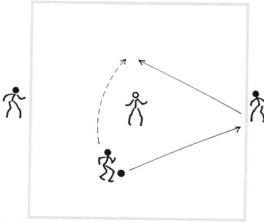

Ex. 13: Dribble and wall pass

COACHING POINTS:
- Encourage players to use the outside of the foot as well as the inside of the foot to pass the ball.
- When the ball is passed to the outside player, the passing player should move quickly to receive the return pass.

Age Range: Suitable for 10/11 years and upwards.

Note: Many of the other exercises in this book will involve inside of the foot passing, especially those in Chapter 14, Creating Space (page 95). It should also be noted that playing small-sided games in training provides absolutely first class passing practice.

EXERCISES TO DEVELOP OUTSIDE OF THE FOOT PASSING

Young players should be encouraged to use the outside of the foot to pass the ball, as it is a pass that can be used in the normal running stride. Some of the exercises used to develop inside of the foot passing can be adapted to develop outside of the foot passing (specifically Exercises 3, 4, 6, 7, 8, 12, 13). The following exercise is also an excellent one for developing outside of the foot passing:

Exercise 14: Angled File Passing
EXERCISE SET-UP:
Arrange players in two groups of three or four about 15 m apart and at an angle to each other (as shown on page 57).

EXERCISE RULES:
The player at the front of one of the lines dribbles the ball for a few metres and then passes it, using the outside of the foot, to the person at the front of the other line, and then joins the back of the opposite queue.

COACHING POINTS:
- Tell your players to strike the ball firmly by locking the ankle.

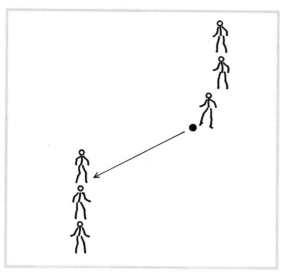

Ex. 14: Angled file passing

Age Range: Suitable for 9/10 years and upwards.

Note: Encourage your players to use the outside of the foot pass in small-sided games and in the exercises used for creating space as outlined in Chapter 14 (page 95).

CHAPTER 10

Shooting

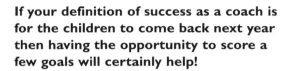

If your definition of success as a coach is for the children to come back next year then having the opportunity to score a few goals will certainly help!

Shooting is one of the fun parts of playing soccer and scoring a goal is a thrill at any level of the game. Although all players can score a goal (even the goalkeeper), there is a far better chance of goals being scored by players playing up the front (strikers or wingers). It is my opinion that all players should be given a go in these positions on a rotational basis until around about 10 years of age.

Coaches should also avoid restricting players to certain parts of the field, for example, not allowing your back four defenders past the halfway line. Soccer is just not played like that anymore and quite often some of these back players are capable of striking the ball extremely well. At top level, goals are being scored by players from a variety of positions.

SHOOTING TECHNIQUE
A player can score a goal with any part of the body, except the hands and arms. In fact top goal scorers do score goals with the toe, head, shins, inside of the foot, outside of the foot, etc. However, a high percentage of goals are scored with what is known as the instep drive technique, as this is the technique which can generate the most powerful strike of the ball.

THE INSTEP DRIVE TECHNIQUE
Basically this is where the ball is struck with the laces of the boot.

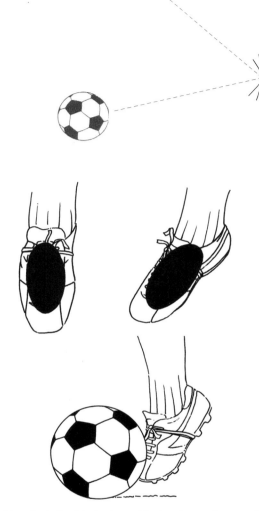

Striking the ball with the laces. Notice the toe is turned slightly outwards; this is so that more of the foot area is in contact with the ball, allowing more control over the direction of the shot

The Instep Drive Technique in Sequence
1. Approach the ball from an angle.
2. Point the shoulder toward the target. (In this case it is the left shoulder pointed towards the target as the player is about to strike the ball with the right foot.)
3. Follow through to the target with the foot still firm.

Note: For a firmer striking surface, tuck the toes up in the sole of the boot, i.e. make a fist with your foot.

PRACTICES FOR INSTEP DRIVE TECHNIQUES

Exercise 1: Instep Drive with a Stationary Ball

Objective: To introduce young players to the basic technique of the instep drive.

EXERCISE SET-UP:

- Each player has a ball up against a fence or a wall.
- If there is no wall or fence available, the players can work in pairs.

EXERCISE RULES:

- The player strikes the ball with the instep.
- If working in pairs, one of the players must keep the sole of his foot on the ball whilst the other player strikes the ball.

Ex. 1: A player practises the instep drive technique with a stationary ball

The sequence for the instep drive. Notice the eyes and head are steady and focused on the ball throughout the sequence

COACHING POINTS:

- Tell the players to strike the ball with the laces (don't expect a perfect technique!).
- Remind the players to tuck their toes up in the sole of the boot of the striking foot.

Age Range: Eight years and upwards.

If a player wants to keep the ball along the ground then he should strike through the centre or top half of the ball. If he wants to get the ball airborne then he should strike through the bottom half of the ball.

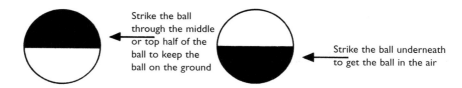

Strike the ball through the middle or top half of the ball to keep the ball on the ground

Strike the ball underneath to get the ball in the air

Exercise 2: Instep Drive in Pairs

Objective: To develop the basic technique of the instep drive.

EXERCISE SET-UP:

- Players are in pairs with a ball between two.
- Each player is approximately 20–25 m away from his partner.

EXERCISE RULES:

Each player pushes the ball to the side, then drives the ball to his partner using the instep drive technique.

Note: The reason the player must push the ball to the side is that striking a slightly moving ball is easier and less daunting than striking a stationary one.

COACHING POINTS:

- Tell the players to tuck their toes up into the bottom of the boot of the striking foot.
- Follow through to the target (in this case the player's partner), with the toes still tucked up in the boot of the striking foot.
- Remind your players to strike through the middle or top half of the ball to keep the ball down.

Age Range: Eight years and upwards.

When the players are confident with this exercise you can introduce the following progression:

Place two markers, 5 m apart, at the midpoint between the two players. Players score a point every time they strike the ball between the markers.

Exercise 3: Shooting in Threes

Objective: To practise the instep drive in a shooting situation.

EXERCISE SET-UP:

- Arrange the players in groups of three.
- An 8-yard goal is marked out for each group of three.
- A few markers are placed approximately 12 m from the marked out goal (this distance varies depending on the age of the players; 12 m is the correct distance for eight- and nine-year-olds to shoot from).

EXERCISE RULES:

- One of the players is the goalkeeper.
- The other two players take it in turns to shoot from either side of the goal.
- The player shooting for goal touches the ball to the side and shoots at goal.
- Rotate the players, with each taking a turn as goalkeeper.

COACHING POINTS:

- Tell the players to tuck their toes up (i.e. make a fist with the foot), into the bottom of the boot of the striking foot.
- Follow through to the target (in this case

Ex. 2: Instep drive in pairs

Ex. 3: Players practise the instep drive by shooting for goal

the goal), with the toes still tucked up in the boot.

■ Remind the players to strike through the middle or top half of the ball, to keep the ball down.

Age Range: Eight years and upwards.

As the players become more proficient in performing the above exercise, the following progressions can be introduced:

(i)   Dribble to shoot: Place three markers through which the players have to dribble before shooting from the 12 m line.
      Age Range: Nine years and upwards.

(ii) Pass to shoot: Mark out a line about 10 m from the 12 m line. The players should be in groups of five. Player A starts at the 10 m line and passes the ball to the feet of Player B, who is stood a few metres away from the 12 m line. Player B lays the pass off into the path of Player A, who shoots first time. This sequence is then repeated on the other side.
      Age Range: 10 years and upwards.

(iii) Corner shooting: Place a marker about 1.5 m inside each 'post' of the 8-yard goal. Ask the players to try striking the ball in between the 'post' and the marker. This will encourage accuracy. You can award 1 point for scoring a goal and 2 points for striking the ball through the markers. This progression can be used for any of the above exercises.
      Age Range: 10 years and upwards.

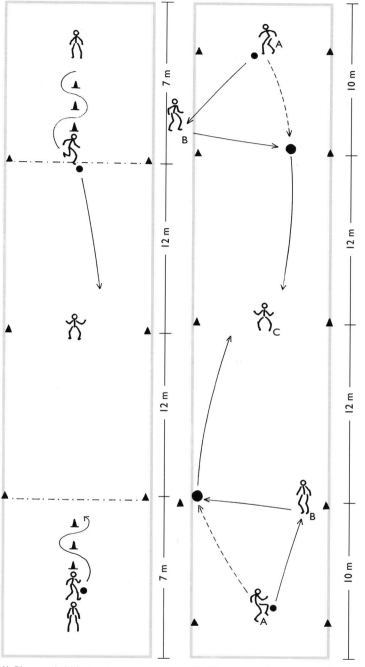

(i) Players dribble to shoot

(ii) Players receive a pass and shoot for goal

Exercise 4: I v. I Goal Scoring

Objective: This is a game-like exercise to combine dribbling and shooting skills.

EXERCISE SET-UP:

- Mark out a number of 8-yard goals and a number of areas about 15 m wide.
- Arrange players in groups of three. One player in goal and two players who will play 1 v. 1 to shoot.

EXERCISE RULES:

- The exercise begins with the two players standing just in front of the goalkeeper.
- The goalkeeper starts the exercise by throwing the ball over the heads of the two players to a distance of approximately 10 m.
- The two players contest the ball to shoot and either player can score.
- Rotate the players at regular intervals.

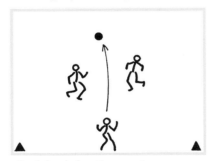

Ex. 4: I v. I shooting practice

COACHING POINTS:

- This is a goal-scoring exercise not a dribbling activity, so the tell players they don't have to beat their opponent to get a shot in.

- Encourage them to get their heads up to look for opportunities to shoot. Try to get them to shoot on sight of goal.

Age Range: Nine years and upwards.

Exercise 5: Chase the Shooter

Objective: To have players practise shooting the ball past the goalkeeper in a game-like situation.

EXERCISE SET-UP:

- Players are arranged in pairs about 25 m from the goal, with a ball between two.
- One of the players is positioned 2–3 m nearer to the goal than his partner.

EXERCISE RULES:

- The coach plays the ball towards goal for the player nearest the goal to shoot.
- The chasing player attempts to win the ball.

COACHING POINTS:

- The player shooting for the goal needs to focus on the ball and the direction of the shot, not on the player chasing him. The player should pick a spot in the goal and aim for it; in many cases this could be just inside the far post.
- Tell the players to strike through the top half of the ball (to keep the ball down).

Note: The coach can vary his pass so the players practise shooting with both feet. He can also throw the ball so players have to volley the ball.

Age Range: Nine/10 years and upwards.

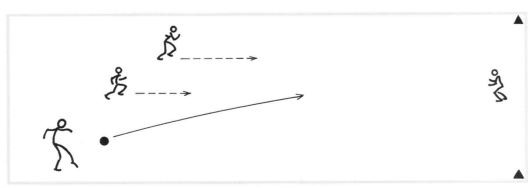

Ex. 5: Shooting under pressure—the coach passes the ball for the player to run onto and shoot

Exercise 6: 2 Attackers v. I Defender

Objective: To combine passing, dribbling and shooting skills in a game-like situation.

EXERCISE SET-UP:

- Mark out an area 15 m wide × 15 m long from the edge of the penalty area.
- Players are in groups of three with one ball per trio.
- The defender starts in a position approximately 10 m from the attackers.

EXERCISE RULES:

- The two attackers have to get the ball past the defender with the aim of scoring a goal.
- The attackers are allowed no more than three passes before they must shoot.
- The attackers may use all of the penalty area.

COACHING POINTS:

- Keep emphasising to the players that they must get the ball past the defender quickly.
- The player with the ball should run at the defender.
- Tell the players to try and score off any rebounds.

Age Range: 10 years and upwards.

Exercise 7: 3 v. 3 Goal Scoring

Objective: The players will learn to score goals not just with the instep drive, but also with the inside of the foot, toe pokes, tap-ins, shots that bend, etc. The exercise is multi-purpose as it will also improve:

- defensive skills
- goalkeeping skills

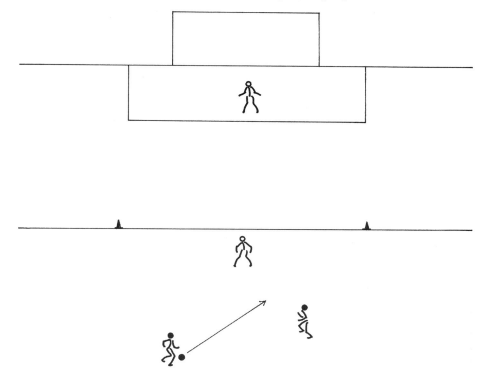

Ex. 6: 2 attackers v. I defender

- decision-making skills
- dribbling skills
- fitness.

EXERCISE SET-UP:

- An 8-yard goal is marked out a few metres outside the penalty area, directly opposite the real goal.
- Markers are placed about 5 m in from the outside of the penalty area. This is done to narrow the width of the penalty area.
- There are six players in the playing area (3 v. 3); three wear coloured bibs to distinguish them from the others.
- There are two goalkeepers (one in each goal).
- There is a ball server next to each of the goals. The game starts when one of the servers passes the ball in to one of the teams.

EXERCISE RULES:

- The aim of the game is simple—each side has to score in the opponents' goal and stop the other side scoring in their goal.
- When a goal is scored, the server next to that goal passes the ball in.
- When the ball goes out of play, it must be served in to the appropriate team (i.e. the team who did not send the ball out of play). There are no throw-ins.
- Players are not allowed to pass the ball back to the goalkeeper. If the keeper saves the ball, he rolls it to one of his team-mates.
- Each game should last approximately 1 to 1½ minutes and then the next group comes on. Each group could have three to five turns each.

COACHING POINTS:

- This is a goal scoring exercise, not a game of 3-a-side. The players are always in shooting range so encourage them to shoot.
- This is a simple exercise to organise and players love it!

Age Range: Eight/nine years and upwards.

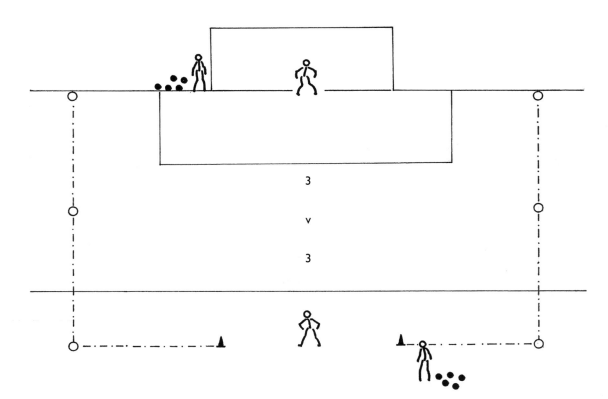

Ex. 7: 3 v 3 goal scoring practice—players love this one

Three attackers against one defender but unfortunately the attackers are too close together

The goalkeeper narrowing the angle to cover the shot on the near post

A quality throw in

Determination to get to the ball first

Striking through the top half of the ball to keep it low

Ouch! Not the best heading technique

Trying to protect the ball under pressure

Eyes up off the ball looking for a teammate

Accelerating between defenders

This player shows excellent awareness by scanning the field of play

Working hard to keep the ball in play

This player needs to get his head up as soon as possible

The chase is on!

Soccer involves physical contact and courage

The defender should win this one

Pass and move – a key factor in good attacking play

Striking the ball on the volley

This player is about to make a decision as to which receiving surface he will use

CHAPTER II
Heading

Young children can be frightened of heading the ball because of the fear of getting hurt. When teaching beginners, the key objective for the coach is to *remove this fear.*

A basic understanding of the technique for heading the ball and the simple eight step coaching progression outlined below will assist you in doing this.

TECHNIQUE FOR HEADING THE BALL

A player should head the ball with the middle of the forehead, keeping the eyes open.

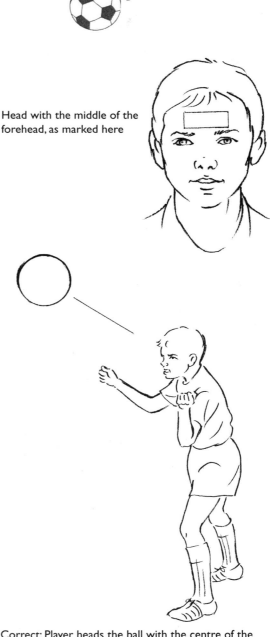

Head with the middle of the forehead, as marked here

Incorrect: Player heads the ball with the nose

Incorrect: Player heads the ball on the top of the head

Correct: Player heads the ball with the centre of the forehead, keeping the eyes open

EIGHT STEPS FOR TEACHING HEADING

You will need to decide at what level of the exercises outlined below your players should begin. For complete beginners definitely start from Step 1 and patiently take them through the progression step by step. If any player finds any step too difficult and starts to head the ball incorrectly (e.g. with the nose or the top of the head), go back a step until confidence is re-established.

Note: When teaching heading to beginners, it is a good idea to let some air out of the balls.

Step 1: Have the players lick their finger and wet the centre of the forehead so they can feel exactly where they are going to head the ball.

Note: At this step or at any subsequent step the coach can go around to each player and press his finger firmly on the centre of each player's forehead for 2 or 3 seconds.

Step 1: Players lick their finger and mark the centre of their forehead

Step 2: Each player has a ball. With the ball in both hands each player gently strikes the ball in the centre of their forehead, ensuring they keep their eyes open throughout.

Step 3: The player can now bring the ball to the forehead more firmly and strike the centre of the ball with the centre of the forehead, then release the ball. This is an excellent

Step 2: Players strike the centre of the forehead with the ball, keeping their eyes open

Step 3: The player brings the ball to his forehead, strikes it with his forehead, at the same time releasing the ball.

exercise as it also encourages the correct use of the arms in the heading technique.

Step 4: Players continue to perform Step 3 but are now in pairs and should aim to head the ball towards their partner's chest. The receiving player then catches the ball.

As the players become more proficient and confident, the 5 m distance can gradually be increased to 10 m.

Note: Step 6 is a significant increase in difficulty from Step 5, so if players experience problems then go back to Steps 4 or 5 until they are ready to progress.

Step 7: Players practise jumping to head the ball. One player holds the ball out for the other player to jump and head.

Step 5: Players hand lob the ball to themselves and head towards their partner's chest

Step 5: Still in pairs, the players hand lob the ball to themselves, and head to their partner.

Step 6: Still in pairs, the players now stand approximately 5 m apart and hand lob the ball for their partner to head back towards the server's chest. Players should have five to 10 turns each and then change.

Step 7: Player holds the ball for his team-mate

Step 6: Players lob the ball to each other

Step 8: In pairs approximately 5–7 m apart, the players lob the ball for their partner to jump and head back towards the server's chest.

Step 8: Players in pairs jump to head the ball

If you follow the above steps your players should have no problems in becoming competent headers of the ball fairly quickly. Take care to progress through the steps at a reasonable pace and avoid spending too long practising heading at any one time. With players aged six to nine you probably should practise only 3–5 minutes at a time, but you could do this on a regular basis and occasionally twice in one training session. For the over-nine age group between 5–7 minutes at a time would be fine.

Note: Most players will not become proficient at Stages 7 and 8 until 10 or 11 years of age.

OTHER PRACTICES FOR HEADING

Note: These exercises are only designed for players who have developed a sound technique and are competent and confident headers of the ball.

Exercise 1: Keep the Ball off the Ground

Objective: To have players develop a feel for the ball when heading.

EXERCISE SET-UP:
Players have a ball each.

EXERCISE RULES:
- Players keep the ball in the air using only their heads.
- Players can count the number of times they can head the ball in the air and always aim to improve their personal best.

Ex. 1: Players keep the ball in the air using only their heads

COACHING POINTS:
- Tell the players to keep their eyes on the ball.
- Tell them to keep alive on the balls of their feet.
- Players should bend at the knees and at the lower back to help control the header.

Note: Make sure players still head the ball with the centre of the forehead.

Age Range: Start this activity as soon as players are competent headers of the ball.

Exercise 2: Heading in Pairs

Objective: To teach players control when heading the ball.

EXERCISE SET-UP:

Players are in groups of two or more.

EXERCISE RULES:

Two or more players keep the ball in the air by heading the ball to each other.

COACHING POINTS:

- The key to success in this exercise is to tell the players to head for height, so their partner has time to move into position to be ready for the return header.
- Players must also bend more at the knees to gain control over the header.

Note: As the ball is coming down from a greater height there is the possibility of heading the ball with the top of the head. Make sure that your players are still heading with the centre of the forehead, keeping their eyes open.

Age Range: Nine years and upwards (but don't expect too much from the average youngster).

Exercise 3: Heading for Goal

Objective: To have players practise heading for goal.

EXERCISE SET-UP:

- Mark out a series of 8-yard goals.
- Have the players in groups of three with one player in the goal (Player A), one player serving the ball (Player B) and one player heading for goal (Player C).

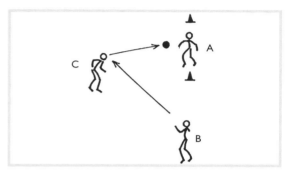

Ex. 3: Players head for goal

EXERCISE RULES:

- Player B hand lobs the ball for Player C to run onto and head for goal.
- Each player has five turns each, and then players rotate positions.
- If the ground is soft then the players can practise diving headers.

Ex. 2: Players heading in pairs

Players heading for goal—kids really love this one!

COACHING POINTS:

- Ensure your players use the centre of the forehead and keep their eyes open.
- When the players are fairly competent, tell them to try keeping the ball down by heading through the top half of the ball, and preferably aiming for the corners of the goal.

Age Range: Eight/nine years and upwards—providing the players are competent headers of the ball.

Exercise 4: Man in the Middle Heading

Objective: To have players practise moving in to head the ball.

EXERCISE SET-UP:

- Arrange players in groups of three.
- The outside players, Player A and Player B, have a ball each and are about 5 m from Player C.

EXERCISE RULES:

- Player A hand lobs to Player C, who heads back to Player A. Player C then turns and heads back a hand lob from Player B, then turns around to head a hand lob serve from Player A and so on.
- The player in the middle (Player C) receives five serves from each of the outside players, then players rotate positions.

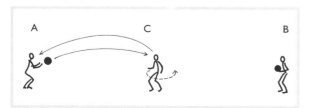

Ex.. 4: Man in the middle heading

- Player C should aim to head the ball towards the chest of the server.

COACHING POINTS:

Tell players to strike through the ball with the centre of the forehead, keeping the eyes open.
Age Range: Nine years and upwards.

Exercise 5: Moving Forwards Heading

Objective: This exercise teaches players to move forward and attack the ball with their heads.

EXERCISE SET-UP:

The players pair off with one ball per pair.

EXERCISE RULES:

- The server (Player A) moves backwards, while the player heading the ball (Player B) moves forwards, facing his partner.
- Player A hand lobs the ball to Player B; Player B moves forward and heads the ball back to his partner's chest.
- Server and header change roles every 30–50 m.

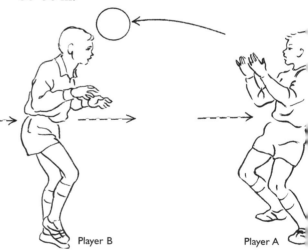

Player B   Player A

Ex. 5: Player B moves forward to attack the ball

COACHING POINTS:

Tell the players to strike through the ball with the centre of the forehead, keeping their eyes open.
Age Range: Nine/10 years and upwards—providing the players are competent headers of the ball.

Exercise 6: Moving Backwards Heading

Objective: To have the players head the ball whilst moving backwards.

EXERCISE SET-UP:

The players pair off with one ball per pair.

EXERCISE RULES:

- The server (Player A) moves forward with the ball and the player heading the ball (Player B) moves backwards, facing his partner.
- Player A hand lobs the ball to Player B.
- Player B heads the ball back to his partner's chest.
- After 30–50 m the server and header change roles and return to the starting point.

COACHING POINTS:

Make sure your players are still striking the ball with the centre of the forehead, keeping their eyes open.

Age Range: 10 years and upwards—this exercise requires a certain amount of strength and agility, so is unsuitable for very young players.

Exercise 7: Angle Heading in a Triangle

Objective: To have players practise redirecting the ball.

EXERCISE SET-UP:

In groups of three the players form a triangle.

EXERCISE RULES:

- Player A hand lobs the ball to Player B, who heads it to Player C; Player C catches the ball and hand lobs it to Player A, who heads the ball to Player B. Player B catches the ball and hand lobs it to Player C and so on.
- This cycle can also be done in reverse.

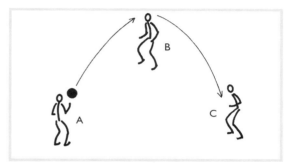

Ex. 7: Players practise redirecting the ball

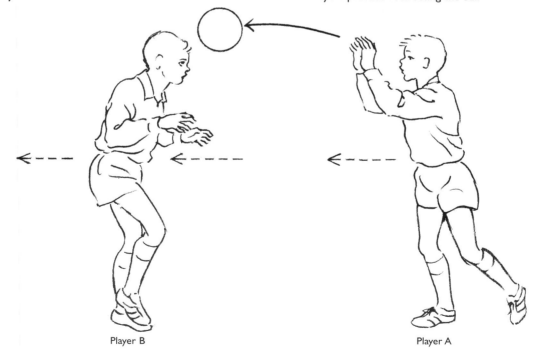

Player B

Player A

Ex. 6: Player B moves backwards, heading the ball back to his partner's chest

COACHING POINTS:

It is crucial that your players still head the ball with the centre of the forehead, not the side of the head. Watch out for this problem.

Age Range: Nine/10 years and upwards—if your players are reasonable headers of the ball.

Exercise 8: The Heading Circle

Objective: A game-like exercise to have the players practise heading and moving.

EXERCISE SET-UP:

- Players form a circle, which should be about 20 m across.
- Move half of the players (in this case six) into the centre of the circle, leaving the remaining players (still forming the circle), with a ball each.

EXERCISE RULES:

- On command, the players in the middle of the circle move and head hand lobs from the players on the outside.

- The player heading the ball should aim it back to the server's chest.
- After about 1 minute, the players on the outside and inside of the circle swap positions.
- When a player has headed a ball he is *not allowed* to go to the person on either side of that server for his next header—this important rule ensures more game-like movements.

COACHING POINTS:

Ensure your players contact the ball with the centre of the forehead, keeping their eyes open.

Age Range: Nine/10 years and upwards—as long as your players are confident and competent headers of the ball.

Exercise 9: Head and Move

Objective: This game-like exercise is aimed at teaching players to:

- look for each other (awareness);

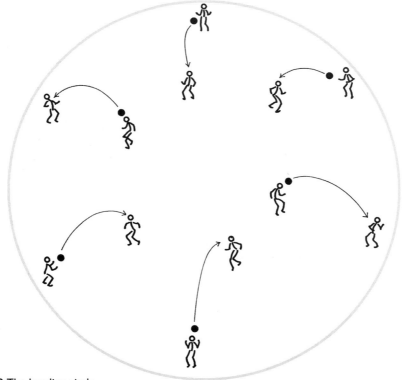

Ex. 8: The heading circle

- time their runs to meet the ball;
- call for the ball;
- direct a header through a crowd of players;
- create space by moving after heading the ball.

EXERCISE SET-UP:

- Mark out a grid as shown by the witch's hats in the diagram below (for 12 players use a grid approximately 20 m × 20 m).
- Place two markers on each of the four sides of the grid and a few metres outside the grid as shown by 'O' in the diagram.
- Players should be in pairs with a ball between two.

EXERCISE RULES:

- Player A dribbles the ball around any one of the outside markers (indicated by 'O' on the diagram); at the same time his partner, Player B, also runs around any outside marker but not on the same side of the grid as Player A.
- When the player with the ball has reached one of the outside markers he picks the ball up and lob serves to his partner running

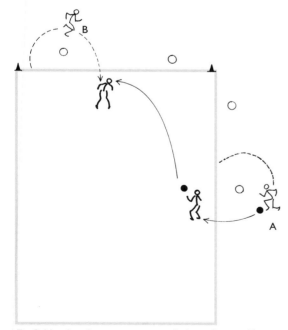

Ex. 9: Head and move, a very realistic and game-like practice

back into the grid who heads the ball back for him to receive and start the sequence again.

- Players change roles after approximately five turns.

As the players become used to this exercise, gradually increase the complexity of the activity by introducing the following rules:

- When both players are running around the outside markers they must keep looking for each other (awareness).
- The player about to head the ball (Player B) must call when he is ready to receive the throw from his partner.
- The player heading the ball must direct the header towards his partner's chest (and always remind them of the Golden Rule of heading—contact the ball with the middle of the forehead, keeping the eyes open).

Note: This is a simple exercise to set up and implement and is definitely worth persisting with for players who have a sound heading technique.

Age Range: 10 years and upwards.

Exercise 10: Throw–Head–Catch

Objective: This game-like exercise provides players with the opportunity to head the ball in a variety of directions, with defenders challenging for the ball. It also encourages other attacking players to support the player heading the ball.

EXERCISE SET-UP:

- Mark out a grid approximately 20 m wide × 25 m long, with a 4 m goal at either end.
- Start out with three players on either side. As players become proficient at this exercise the player numbers and the size of the pitch can be increased.

EXERCISE RULES:

- The side in possession of the ball may only follow the sequence throw–head–catch in order to progress towards their goal.
- If the ball touches the ground the last team to have touched it loses possession.

- Defenders have to intercept in sequence; i.e. if the opposition has just thrown the ball they must intercept the pass by heading, if the opposition have just headed the ball they must intercept by catching.
- Goals can only be scored with a header.

COACHING POINTS:

Every time a player throws the ball to a team-mate he must move into position to catch the return header.

Age Range: 10 years and upwards —as long as your players are confident and competent headers of the ball.

Note: Before using any of the previous exercises please ensure that your players are confident and competent headers of the ball. If they aren't, then focus on the 'Eight Steps for Teaching Heading' (page 66).

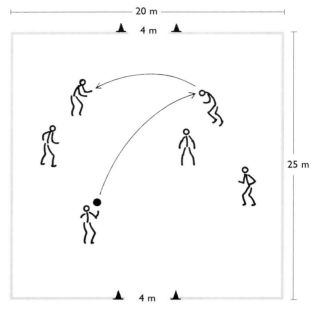

Ex. 10: Throw–head–catch game

CHAPTER 12
Receiving the Ball

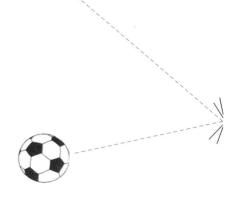

Being able to bring the ball under control quickly is critical to becoming a good soccer player.

There are two main reasons why great players always have so much time on the ball:
1. They position themselves to create maximum space away from the nearest defender.
2. They bring the ball under control quickly, therefore creating time for themselves.

KEY COACHING POINTS IN RECEIVING THE BALL

The following coaching points apply irrespective of which part of the body the player is using to receive the ball. To receive the ball the player should:

Point 1: Move behind the line of flight of the ball as early as possible; i.e. move his feet to get his body behind the ball, then **slow down** just prior to receiving the ball and be balanced and calm.

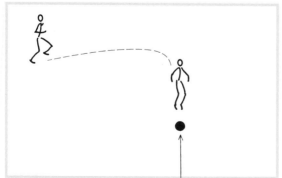

The player moves behind the line of flight of the ball and slows down just prior to impact

Point 2: Offer the receiving surface towards the ball.

Point 3: Withdraw the receiving surface just before the ball makes contact.

LEFT The player offers the receiving surface, in this case the thigh, towards the ball
RIGHT The player withdraws the receiving surface

Coaching Phrases: The coach can also encourage the player to receive the ball correctly by delivering the following coaching phrases in a fairly soft and relaxed tone: 'Relax', 'Be soft', 'Imagine your body is a sponge', 'Give', 'Go floppy', 'Absorb the impact', 'Slow down'.

The most frequently used receiving surface for gaining control of a ball travelling *along the ground* is:

(i) Inside of the foot

(ii) The Thigh

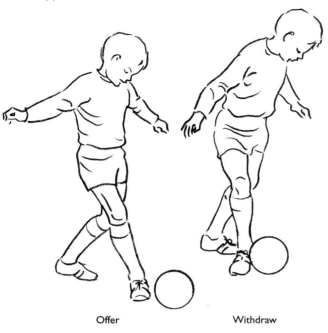

Offer   Withdraw

Offer

Withdraw

The most frequently used receiving surfaces for gaining control of a ball travelling *through the air* are:

(i) The Instep (this is the top part of the foot, i.e. the laces on the boot)

(iii) The Chest

When receiving the ball with the chest, the crucial action of the receiver is to bend at the

Offer   Withdraw

LEFT The player bends at the knees and the ball bounces in the air off the chest

RIGHT The player now brings the ball under control with either foot

knees and the lower part of the back to absorb the impact. The ball will bounce in the air slightly off the chest and the player will need to use another surface (such as the instep), if he wants to keep possession of the ball.

TRAPPING THE BALL TECHNIQUE

Trapping the ball is a different technique from receiving the ball. The player controls the ball by trapping it on the half volley, using the inside or outside of the foot. The player squeezes the ball into the ground by playing through the top half of the ball with his knee over the top of the ball.

Trapping the ball: the player squeezes the ball into the ground. Notice the knee is well over the ball

EXERCISES FOR RECEIVING THE BALL ON THE GROUND

Exercise 1: Pairs

Objective: To practise receiving the ball with the inside of the foot.

EXERCISE SET-UP:

Players stand facing each other approximately 10 m apart.

EXERCISE RULES:

The players pass the ball to each other using the inside of the foot and receive the ball using the inside of the foot.

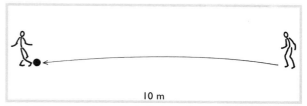

Ex. 1: Players receiving the ball along the ground with the inside of the foot

COACHING POINTS:

- Players must keep alive on the balls of the feet but at the same time be relaxed.
- Use coaching phrases to encourage control such as 'Relax,' 'Let the foot go floppy', etc.

Age Range: Seven/eight years.

As your players become proficient in this exercise, have them try receiving with one foot and passing with the other.

Exercise 2: Pairs on the Move

Objective: To practise receiving the ball whilst on the move.

EXERCISE SET-UP:

- Players are in pairs, with a ball per pair.
- Each pair is stationed near a marker.
- Each player stands approximately 12 m away from his partner.

EXERCISE RULES:

- Player A starts at the marker, moves forward to receive the ball with the inside of the foot, passes back to Player B and runs back around the marker.
- Player A repeats the sequence for about a minute, then Player B has a turn.

COACHING POINTS:

- Tell players to slow down just before receiving the ball.

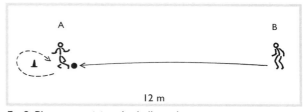

Ex. 2: Players receiving the ball on the move

- Use coaching phrases such as 'Relax', 'Let the foot give with the ball' to create the right atmosphere.

Age Range: Eight/nine years and upwards.

As your players become proficient in this exercise, have them try receiving with one foot and passing with the other.

Exercise 3: Receive, Pass, Turn

Objective: To introduce a more game-like aspect to receiving the ball.

EXERCISE SET-UP:

Arrange players in groups of three in straight lines (Player A, Player B, Player C), with about 7 m between each player.

EXERCISE RULES:

- Player A passes to Player B, who receives the ball with the inside of the foot and makes a return pass to Player A. Player B then turns to face Player C and the same sequence occurs.
- Players should change positions approximately every minute.

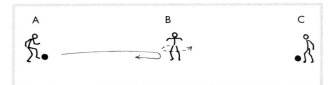

Ex. 3: Receive, pass, turn

COACHING POINTS:

Use coaching phrases such as 'Relax', 'Let the foot give with the ball', etc. to create the correct atmosphere.

Age Range: Eight/nine years and upwards.

Exercise 4: Receive and Turn
(using the inside of the foot)

Objective: To have players practise receiving and turning with the ball.

EXERCISE SET-UP:

Arrange players in groups of three in straight lines (Player A, Player B, Player C), with about 7 m between each player.

EXERCISE RULES:

- Player A passes to Player B who receives and turns with the ball (using the inside of the foot), and passes to Player C. Player C then passes to Player B and the same sequence is repeated.
- Make sure players practise with both feet.
- Players should change positions approximately every minute.

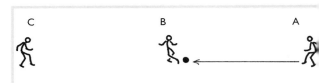

Ex. 4: Players receive and turn with the ball using the inside of the foot

COACHING POINTS:

- The player in the middle (Player B), should be nearly sideways on (i.e. in a half-turned position) to both outside players and able to see both outside players. Keep on asking the player in the middle if he can see both outside players.
- Emphasise that the receiving player should be balanced, calm and relaxed.

Age Range: Suitable for 9 years and upwards.

Note: Players can also try the above exercise using the outside of the foot.

Exercise 5: Receive and Move

Objective: This game-like exercise is aimed at teaching players to:

- look for each other (awareness)
- time their runs to meet the ball
- call for the ball
- control the ball into space

EXERCISE SET-UP:

- Mark out a grid as shown by the witch's hats in the diagram on page 79. For 12 players the grid should be about 20 m × 20 m.
- Place two markers on each of the four sides of the grid and a few metres outside of the grid as shown by the symbol 'O' in the diagram.

- Players should be in pairs with a ball between two.

EXERCISE RULES:

- Player A dribbles the ball around any one of the outside markers (O); at the same time his partner (Player B), also runs around any outside marker but not on the same side of the grid as his partner with the ball.
- When Player A has dribbled around one of the outside markers (O), he passes the ball to Player B (who is running back into the grid). Player B receives the ball with the inside or outside of the foot, turns, and dribbles the ball around a different outside marker, and the sequence is repeated.

Once the players are confident with this exercise you can introduce the following rules:

- When both players are running around the outside markers they must keep looking for each other (awareness).
- The player without the ball must call when he is ready to receive the pass from his partner.

The following progression can be introduced along with the above rules:

The coach can move into the grid, and act as a defender by challenging the players as they are about to receive the ball. This will encourage the players to control the ball into space. The challenge from the coach should not be at all threatening or physical.

COACHING POINTS:

- Tell the players to slow down just prior to receiving the ball.

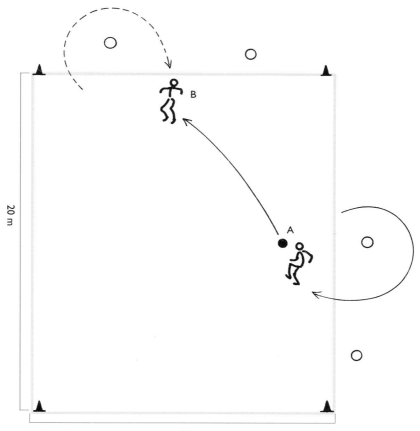

20 m

20 m

Ex. 5: Receive and move

- Use coaching phrases such as 'Relax', 'Be calm', 'Let the foot go floppy', to create the right atmosphere.

Age Range: 10 years and upwards.

Note: This is a very simple exercise to set up and implement and is definitely worth persisting for players who have a fairly good receiving technique.

EXERCISES FOR RECEIVING THE BALL IN THE AIR

Exercise 6: Self-Serve Air Ball

Objective: To bring the falling ball under control

EXERCISE SET-UP:

- For 12 players mark out a grid approximately 15 m × 10 m.
- Each player has a ball.

EXERCISE RULES:

The players throw the balls in the air towards themselves and practise receiving it with a variety of surfaces such as the instep, thigh, chest, as well as the inside of the foot trap.

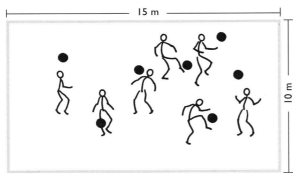

Ex. 6: Players serve and receive the ball

COACHING POINTS:

Use coaching phrases such as 'Feel yourself going floppy', 'Relax', 'Be like a sponge', 'Be balanced'.

Age Range: Seven/eight years and upwards.

Note: Young players can let the ball bounce first and then receive the ball.

Exercise 7: Self-Serve Air Ball and Move

Objective: This is a game-like progression of Exercise 6. It helps players develop their awareness of where the other players are whilst the ball is in the air; they also learn to receive the ball into space away from other players.

EXERCISE SET-UP:

For 12 players mark out a grid 15 m × 10 m, with two additional markers placed just outside and on each side of the grid.

EXERCISE RULES:

- Each player throws the ball in the air towards himself, receiving it with a variety of surfaces such as the instep, thigh, chest, and inside of the foot trap.
- Each player then dribbles the ball around one of the outside markers back into the grid, and repeats the sequence.

Ex. 7: Players receive the ball and dribble around a marker

COACHING POINTS:

- Tell the players to look out for each other.
- Use coaching phrases such as 'Feel yourself going floppy', 'Relax', 'Be still'.

Age Range: Eight years and upwards.

When the players are confident with this exercise you can introduce the following progression:

The coach can move into the grid, act as a defender and challenge players as they are about to receive the ball. This will encourage the players to control the ball into the space away from the defender. The challenge from the coach should not be at all threatening or physical.

Age Range: Avoid introducing this progression until the players are reasonably competent at receiving the ball. They don't have to be perfect, just reasonably competent.

Exercise 8: Individual Ball Juggling

Objective: To develop balance and a feel for the ball.

EXERCISE SET-UP:

One ball per player.

EXERCISE RULES:

Each player keeps the ball in the air for as many touches as possible, using any part of the body except the arms.

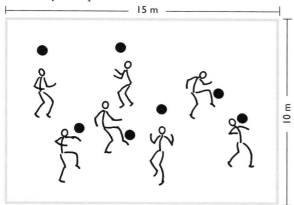

Ex. 8: Players ball juggling

COACHING POINTS:

■ Tell players to be relaxed, calm and balanced but alive on the balls of their feet.
■ Tell the players to keep their eyes on the ball.

Age Range: Open—players can practise ball juggling at any age. Young players should be encouraged to practise at home. In fact this can be homework on a regular basis. Have the players count the number of consecutive times they can keep the ball in the air.

Note: Ball juggling can also be practised in between exercises at training and by those players who arrive early.

Exercise 9: Pairs

Objective: To practise receiving the ball with various parts of the body

EXERCISE SET-UP:

■ For 12 players, mark out a grid 15 m × 15 m.
■ Players stand facing each other in the grid, approximately 5 m apart.

EXERCISE RULES:

One player uses a two-handed serve to lob the ball to his team-mate, who receives the ball using the instep, thigh or chest, and then passes back to the feet of server.

Note: Young players can let the ball bounce and then practise their receiving techniques.

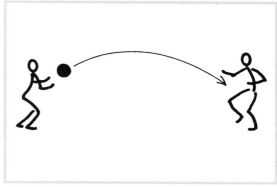

Ex. 9: Players receiving an aerial ball in pairs

COACHING POINTS:

■ The player about to receive the ball must keep alive on the balls of their feet and get their body behind the ball.
■ Use coaching phrases to encourage control such as 'Give', 'Relax', etc.

Age Range: Eight/nine years and upwards.

When the players are confident with this exercise you can introduce the following rule:

The player who has just served the ball must move off 3 m to the side; this allows the player receiving the ball to develop awareness. This exercise should involve all the players in a grid.

Exercise 10: Pairs on the Move

Objective: To practise receiving the ball on the move.

EXERCISE SET-UP:

- Place the markers as per the diagram below.
- Players stand approximately 10 m apart.
- Player A starts at the marker; Player B hand lobs the ball in the air. Player A moves forward to receive the ball. After receiving the ball, Player A passes back to Player B and runs back around the marker to repeat the same sequence.

Ex. 10: The player moves forward to receive the ball using the thigh, chest or instep

COACHING POINTS:

- Tell the players to move their bodies behind the ball.
- Tell the players to *slow down* just before receiving the ball.
- Use coaching phrases such as 'Relax', 'Slow down', 'Give with the ball', etc.

Age Range: Nine/10 years and upwards.

Exercise 11: Ball Juggling in Pairs

Objective: To develop a sense of touch and feel for receiving the ball in the air.

EXERCISE SET-UP:

The players pair off and stand approximately 5 m apart.

EXERCISE RULES:

- Working in their pairs the players must pass the ball to each other, keeping it off the ground.
- Initially the players may use as many touches as they like to receive and then pass the ball back to their team-mate. As soon as they become competent the coach

Ex. 11: Two players keep the ball in the air

can insist they use only two touches; i.e. one touch to receive the ball and one to pass back to their partner.

COACHING POINTS:

- Players need to be alive on the balls of their feet and move their body behind the ball.
- Use coaching phrases such as 'Relax', 'Be soft', 'Be balanced', etc.

Age Range: 10 years and upwards.

Note: This exercise can also involve three, four or five players keeping the ball in the air and is another good exercise to use in between other exercises at training.

Exercise 12: Receiving in Threes

Objective: To receive the ball in a more mobile situation.

EXERCISE SET-UP:

- Arrange players in groups of three (Player A, Player B and Player C), with each player in a straight line and about 5 m between each player.
- Player A and Player C have a ball each.

EXERCISE RULES:

- Player A lobs the ball by hand to Player B, who receives the ball and makes a return pass to Player A. Player B then turns to face Player C, and the same sequence is repeated.
- Players should change positions approximately every minute.

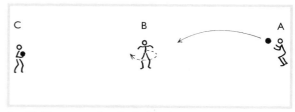

Ex. 12: Players receive the ball and turn

COACHING POINTS:
Use coaching phrases such as 'Stay calm', 'Be balanced', etc. to create the correct atmosphere. *Age Range*: Nine/10 years and upwards.

Exercise 13: Receive and Turn
Objective: To have players practise receiving the ball in the air and turning with the ball.
EXERCISE SET-UP:
Arrange players in groups of three (Player A, Player B and Player C) in straight lines, with about 5 m between each player.
EXERCISE RULES:
- Player A lobs the ball by hand to Player B, who receives and turns with the ball to pass to Player C. Player C then lobs to Player B and the sequence is repeated.
- Players should change positions approximately every minute.
COACHING POINTS:
- The receiving player (Player B) should be nearly sideways on to both outside players

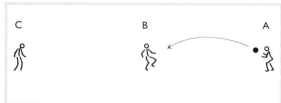

Ex. 13: Player B receives the ball and turns in the same movement

(i.e. in a half turned position) and able to see both players.
- Keep asking Player B if he can see Player A and Player C.
- Emphasise that the receiving player (Player B) should be balanced, calm, relaxed and relatively still when he receives the ball.
Age Range: Nine/10 years and upwards.

Exercise 14: The Circle
Objective: A game-like exercise to teach players to receive the ball in the air, pass, then move.
EXERCISE SET-UP:
- Ask players to form a circle. For 12 players the circle should be about 20 m across.
- Move half of the players into the centre of the circle leaving the remaining players still forming the circle and with a ball each.
EXERCISE RULES:
- On command, the players in the middle of the circle move to receive a hand serve from one of the players on the outside; they must then control the ball using the chest or thigh and pass the ball back to the server. The pass can be on the ground aimed at the feet of the server, or on the volley to the chest of the server.
- After about one minute, the players on the inside and the outside of the circle change over.
- When a player has received and passed the ball he is not allowed to go to the person on either side of that server for his next serve. This important rule ensures more game-like movements.

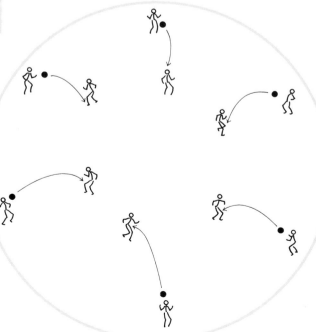

RIGHT Ex. 14: Players practise receive, pass, move

COACHING POINTS:

- Tell players to *slow down* just prior to receiving the ball.
- Tell players to get their body behind the ball.
- Use coaching phrases such as 'Just give with the ball', 'Be calm and relaxed'.

Age Range: 10/11 years and upwards.

Exercise 15: Receive and Move

Objective: This game-like exercise is aimed at teaching players to:

- look for each other (awareness);
- time their runs to meet the ball;
- call for the ball;
- control the ball into space.

EXERCISE SET-UP:

- Mark out a grid as shown by the witch's hats in the diagram below. For 12 players the grid should be about 20 m × 20 m.

- Place two markers on each of the four sides of the grid and a few metres outside of the grid as shown by the symbol 'O' in the diagram.
- Players should be in pairs with a ball between two.

EXERCISE RULES:

- Player A dribbles the ball around any one of the outside markers (O); at the same time his partner (Player B) also runs around any outside marker but not on the same side of the grid as his partner with the ball.
- When Player A has reached one of the outside markers (O), he picks the ball up and hand lobs the ball to Player B, who is now running back into the grid. Player B receives the ball with the instep, thigh or chest; he turns, dribbles the ball around a different outside marker, and the sequence is repeated.

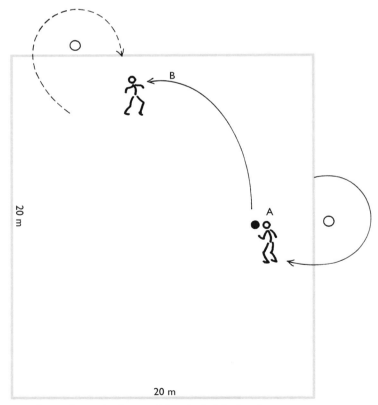

Ex. 15: Receive and move—an advanced practice for receiving the ball in the air

COACHING POINTS:

- Tell players to get their body behind the ball as early as possible and to *slow down* just prior to receiving the ball.
- Use coaching phrases such as 'Relax', 'Be calm', 'Give with the ball' to create the right atmosphere.

Age Range: 10/11 years and upwards.

As the players become used to the above exercise, introduce these rules:

- When both players are running around the outside markers they must keep looking for each other (awareness).
- The player about to receive the ball must call when he is ready to receive the throw from his partner.

Once the players have become reasonably competent, try introducing this progression:

The coach can move into the grid and act as a defender by challenging the players as they are about to receive the ball. This will encourage them to control the ball into space. The coach should avoid appearing threatening or physically intimidating; any contact or tackling would not benefit the exercise.

Note: This is a very simple exercise to set up and implement and is definitely worth persisting with for players who have fairly good receiving technique.

CHAPTER 13
Goalkeeping

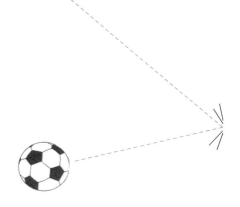

Goalkeepers are not soccer players!
They are specialist players who have to learn a totally different set of skills. Unlike an outfield player they don't have to develop expertise in receiving the ball on the thigh, chest or instep, and they don't have to learn how to shoot or dribble, however they do have to learn how to use their hands!

All children up to the age of about nine or 10 should be allowed to have a regular turn in goal. By age 10 there will probably be one or two players in the team who are putting their hand up to play in goal on a regular basis. This section is aimed at assisting these players become better goalkeepers by looking at the basic techniques only.

Players who are serious about their goalkeeping skills need to receive specialist coaching from a coach who has played as a goalkeeper.

GOALKEEPING, THE BASIC POSITION
Feet—shoulder-width apart
Legs—knees slightly bent
Body—leans slightly forward
Hands—palms facing the ball, fingers widespread and pointing upward
Weight—slightly forward towards the balls of the feet
Eyes—focused on the ball
Arms—in front of the body, elbows well bent, forearms widespread and pointing upward

GET THE BODY BEHIND THE BALL
One of the keys to successful goalkeeping is to always get as much of the body behind the ball as possible. This requires goalkeepers to have quick foot movements and to use these quick foot movements to move behind the line of flight of the ball as quickly as possible. They also need to be able to absorb the impact of the ball with 'soft hands' and/or 'give' in the body. This applies whether the keeper is catching the ball or stopping a shot.

THE SAFE AND SECURE POSITION
Another key to successful goalkeeping is for the goalkeeper to bring the ball to the *Safe and Secure Position* on every occasion after he has caught the ball or stopped a shot. Goalkeepers of all ages and levels should practise this in training so it becomes a habit.

The Basic Goalkeeping Position

LEFT The *Safe and Secure Position*; the goalkeeper has the
ball firmly encased to the chest
RIGHT The Stoop Technique

GOALKEEPING TECHNIQUES

Catching the Low Ball along the Ground: The Stoop Technique

To receive a low ball the goalkeeper:
- bends forward from the waist;
- lowers the hands, turning palms upwards;
- As the ball passes over the palms and onto the forearms, the goalkeeper bends the elbows to encase the ball between his arms and the body. He then straightens his body to an upright position with the ball firmly secured in the Safe and Secure Position.

Catching the Low Ball along the Ground: The Drop to the Knee Technique

To receive a low ball using this technique the goalkeeper:
- drops to one knee, with the knee flush with the foot of the other leg;
- makes sure the chest is facing the direction of the ball;
- lowers the hands, turning the palms upwards;
- As the ball passes over the palms and onto the forearms, the goalkeeper bends the

elbows to encase the ball between the arms and the body. He then straightens his body to an upright position with the ball in the Safe and Secure Position.

Two goalkeepers can practise both of the above methods in pairs with a hand serve along the ground. As they become competent they can serve the ball to each other using an inside of the foot pass.

Catching Medium High Balls: Stomach and Lower Chest Level

This technique is used for shots coming to the goalkeeper at stomach or chest height. Players move their feet to get their body behind the

ball, offer their arms to the ball, let the ball come into the stomach and then firmly hold the ball in the Safe and Secure Position. A key point here is for the goalkeeper to 'give' with the body just prior to receiving the ball.

Two goalkeepers can practise this in pairs using a hand throw and then progress to a volley serve.

Catching Medium High Balls: Higher Chest and Face Level

Position of hands on the ball

The player moves his feet to get his body behind the ball, offers his hands to the ball and lets the hands 'give' to receive the ball. The player then transfers the ball into the Safe and Secure Position.

Goalkeepers can practise this in pairs using a hand throw, then progress to a volley serve.

Catching High Balls

The technique for catching a high ball is exactly the same as the one for catching medium high balls at higher chest and face level but this time the goalkeeper must jump for the ball.

To jump, the goalkeeper takes a long stride with his jumping leg, lifts the knee of his other leg in front of his body, pushes off

Catching a high ball

powerfully with the jumping leg and moves his hands upward towards the ball.

The ball should be caught at the peak of the jump and once it has been caught, the ball should be brought to the Safe and Secure Position. Two goalkeepers can practise this in pairs by lobbing the ball to each other.

FALLING TO SAVE SHOTS: A FOUR STEP TEACHING PROGRESSION

One of the most difficult shots to save is the shot which is on the ground and close to the goalkeeper. Goalkeepers should not dive for these shots as they would probably dive over the top of the ball; instead, they should fall on the ball.

The following steps are simple progressions for teaching budding goalkeepers to fall and save shots; these steps will remove any fear the player has of falling to the ground. The goal-

The *Basic Fallen Position*: the key point is for the goalkeeper to keep the chest facing the ball

keeper should finish each step in the *Basic Fallen Position*, with his chest facing the ball. Repeat each step until the player is competent and confident before moving to the next step.

Step 1:
- The goalkeeper is in a sitting position with the legs straight.
- The server rolls the ball on the ground about half a metre to the side of the sitting player, who just falls over onto his shoulder and allows the ball to come into his chest, wrapping his arms around the ball in the Basic Fallen Position.

Step 2:
- The goalkeeper adopts a kneeling position.
- The server rolls the ball on the ground about half a metre to the side of the kneeling player, who falls over onto his shoulder and allows the ball to come into his chest, wrapping his arms around the ball in the Basic Fallen Position.

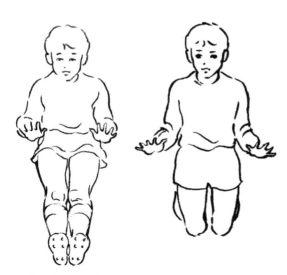

LEFT **Step 1: The sitting position**
RIGHT **Step 2: The kneeling position**

Step 3:
- The goalkeeper now adopts a squatting or semi-crouch position.

- The server rolls the ball on the ground half a metre to the side of the goalkeeper, who falls onto his shoulder and allows the ball to come into his chest, wrapping his arms around the ball in the Basic Fallen Position.

Step 3: The squatting position

Note: To ensure the goalkeeper falls over and doesn't dive, tell him to *collapse* the leg nearest to the ball. Use phrases like 'Let your leg go like jelly', 'Let your leg go from under you', 'Just collapse the leg', etc.

Step 4:
- The goalkeeper now adopts the *Basic Goalkeeping Position* (see page 86).
- The server rolls the ball on the ground about half a metre to one side of the goalkeeper, who *collapses* the leg nearest to the ball, falls onto his shoulder and allows the ball to come into his chest, wrapping his arms around the ball in the Basic Fallen Position.

As the player develops confidence and competence, firmer hand serves can be delivered. Later, foot serves using the inside of the foot and the instep drive can be made.

POSITIONAL PLAY
The goalkeeper should be thinking constantly about his position in relation to his goal and where the ball is on the field of play. This

positional play is critical in the goalkeeper's role as a shot-stopper.

In Diagram 1 below, the attacking player with the ball is on the edge of the penalty area and about to shoot. The goalkeeper is stood on the goal line in the middle of the goal. Given that the goal is 8 yards wide, the goalkeeper's position gives the attacking player the **full width** of the goal to shoot at, and if the shot is directed just inside either post then the keeper has to make a spectacular dive to save the ball. For most young goalkeepers saving such a shot would be impossible.

In Diagram 2 below, the attacking player is in exactly the same position as in Diagram 1 but the goalkeeper has narrowed the shooting angle of the attacker.

By advancing off his goal line the keeper has reduced the size of the attacking player's shooting target. He has also reduced the distance he has to dive to save exactly the same shot from the attacking player.

When narrowing the angle the goalkeeper should:

- advance in the Basic Goalkeeping Position;
- be fairly still (but alive on the balls of the feet), just prior to the ball being struck. The reason for this is that it's hard to push off to the side when moving forward.

Practice for Narrowing the Angle

It is important that the goalkeeper fully understands the principle of narrowing the shooting angle. There are two steps to teaching this:

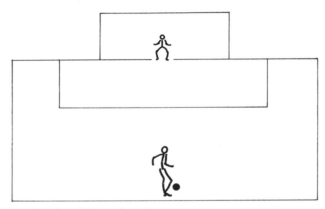

Diagram 1: The attacking player has the whole goal to shoot at

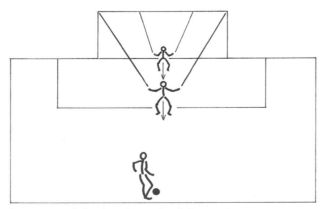

Diagram 2: The goalkeeper has narrowed the shooting angle of the attacker

Step 1: Ask the goalkeeper to stand in the middle of the goal, lie down and try to touch the ball which has been placed just inside the post. This will show him he has virtually no chance of reaching a well-struck shot in the corner of the goal (see Diagram 3 below).

Step 2: The next step is to have the keeper come to the edge of the 6-yard box. Ask him to take up a position from where he believes he could save a ball struck on either side and heading just inside the post. Now place two markers in line with the ball and the posts. In effect, this is the keeper's 'new goal' (see Diagram 4 below).

Ask him to lie down and see if he can touch or nearly touch a ball placed just inside the markers.

He should be able to touch the ball on both sides of this new goal. He can now reach a shot directed inside the post and will understand the importance of narrowing the shooting angle.

Once your goalkeeper understands the importance of narrowing the shooting angle, you can try introducing the following progressions:

(i) The coach moves around just inside the penalty area with the ball at his feet; the goalkeeper must constantly reposition himself.

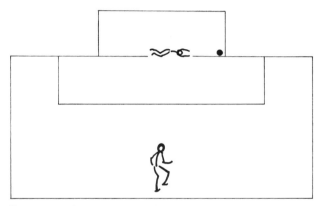

Diagram 3: Having the goalkeeper stand in the middle of the goal and then lie down to try and reach the corners shows him he has little or no chance of reaching the ball

Diagram 4: The goalkeeper lies down to touch the ball

At intervals the coach can shout 'Stop' and the goalkeeper has to freeze on the spot. The coach then places two markers in line between the ball and the posts to mark the keeper's new goal. The coach then:

(a) asks the player lie down on his side and see if he can reach or nearly reach the markers (which represent the post of the new goal), with an outstretched arm;

(b) stands in the footsteps of the goalkeeper and lets the goalkeeper stand over the ball to assess the quality of his positional play.

(ii) takes some shots from different angles (or a player if the coach has never played the game), the keeper attempts to narrow the shooting angle in response (Diagram 5).

Age Range: 10 years and upwards (for specialist goalkeepers).

ADDITIONAL GOALKEEPER EXERCISES

The following exercises can be introduced with goalkeepers from the age of 10/11.

Individual Work

Exercise 1: Developing a Feel for the Ball

Objective: To encourage novice goalkeepers to develop a feel for the ball.

EXERCISE SET-UP:
One ball per goalkeeper.

EXERCISE RULES:
The goalkeeper moves around bouncing the ball on the ground, first with the right hand and then the left hand.

COACHING POINTS:
Emphasise to your keepers that they must use their fingers and not the palms of their hands.

Exercise 2: Catching High Balls

Objective: For the goalkeeper to practise positioning his body correctly for catching high balls.

EXERCISE SET-UP:
One ball per goalkeeper.

EXERCISE RULES:
The goalkeeper bounces the ball into the ground, then jumps to catch the ball; his arms should be outstretched above his head and slightly in front of his body.

Exercise 3: Improving Agility

Objective: To improve agility in players.

EXERCISE SET-UP:
One ball per goalkeeper.

EXERCISE RULES:
The keeper throws the ball in the air, performs a forward or backward roll (somersault), then catches the ball.

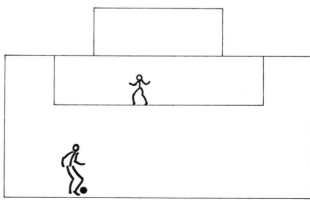

Diagram 5: Narrowing the angle: the coach takes shots from different angles.

Exercise 4: Developing Reactions

Objective: To increase the speed of the goalkeeper's reactions.

EXERCISE SET-UP:

One ball per goalkeeper.

EXERCISE RULES:

The goalkeeper lies on his back, throws the ball in the air away from his body, and has to either dive or jump to his feet to catch the ball before it hits the ground.

Goalkeepers Working in Pairs

Exercise 5: Developing Ball Handling Skills

Objective: To improve ball handling skills.

EXERCISE SET-UP:

Two goalkeepers, with a ball between them.

EXERCISE RULES:

- Goalkeeper A sits on the ground with his legs apart and in front of him.
- Goalkeeper B stands about 3 m away and throws the ball at different heights and to either side of Goalkeeper A for him to catch and throw back.

Exercise 6: Developing Reactions

Objective: To increase the speed of the goalkeeper's reactions.

EXERCISE SET-UP:

Two goalkeepers, with a ball between them.

EXERCISE RULES:

- Goalkeeper A stands with his legs apart, facing his partner (Goalkeeper B) at a distance of approximately 2 m.
- Goalkeeper B acts as a server and rolls the ball between his partner's legs; Goalkeeper A turns and dives for the ball.

Exercise 7: Catching High Balls on the Move

Objective: To practise catching high balls in a game-like situation.

EXERCISE SET-UP:

Two goalkeepers, with a ball between them.

EXERCISE RULES:

The two goalkeepers face each other and as Goalkeeper A runs backwards, Goalkeeper B moves forwards and lobs the ball just over his team-mate's head, forcing Goalkeeper A to jump and catch the ball.

Exercise 8: Shot Stopping High Lobs

Objective: To practise stopping high balls in the goal.

EXERCISE SET-UP:

Two goalkeepers, with a ball between them.

EXERCISE RULES:

- Goalkeeper A stands in the middle of the goal, with Goalkeeper B facing him about 10 m away.
- Goalkeeper A runs to a marker at the edge of the 6 yard box; just as he reaches the marker his teammate lobs the ball over his head to either side.
- Goalkeeper A makes every attempt to make the save.

Exercise 9: Improving Shot Stopping and Diving

Objective: To develop goalkeeping skills in the goal.

EXERCISE SET-UP:

Two goalkeepers, with a ball between them.

EXERCISE RULES:

Another goal is set up 10–20 m away from the main goal. The keepers now try and score by throwing the ball in the other keeper's goal.

Exercise 10: Improving Shot Stopping, Reactions and Agility

Objective: To develop goalkeeping skills in the goal.

EXERCISE SET-UP:

Two goalkeepers, with a ball between them.

EXERCISE RULES:

- Goalkeeper A stands in the centre of the goal. Goalkeeper B acts as a server and stands about 10 m away with a number of balls.

- Goalkeeper B serves the ball high to one side of Goalkeeper A for him to save, then serves a low ball to the other side for him to save.

Exercise 11: Developing Reactions

Objective: To develop the goalkeeper's reactions in the goal area.

EXERCISE SET-UP:

Two goalkeepers, with a ball between them.

EXERCISE RULES:

- Goalkeeper A stands in the middle of the goal facing the net. Goalkeeper B (the server) stands about 15 m away.
- Goalkeeper B throws the ball in the direction of goal, but just before he throws the ball he shouts 'turn'.
- Goalkeeper A (standing on the line) turns and attempts to save the ball.

COACHING POINTS:

The server should mix up the serves—some low, some high, some soft, some hard, etc.

Note: Some of these exercises are physically demanding and should only be done with young players in short bursts, say 30 seconds at a time for each exercise.

Also remember that goalkeepers can be involved in most aspects of training, whether that be in the shooting exercises or by having larger goals in the small-sided games.

CHAPTER 14

Creating Space

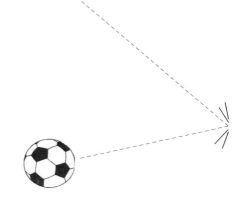

One of the most crucial aspects in effective teamwork is that the player in possession of the ball always has a number of team-mates in good positions to receive a pass. This chapter is about getting into a position to receive a pass from a team-mate.

The ability for attacking players to move into position for receiving passes does not come naturally to young players; like any other skill it has to be learned over a period of time. In fact, at the ages of six and seven soccer players chase and crowd around the ball like bees around a honey pot just trying to get a kick; unfortunately there is not too much you can do about this!

Telling them to 'Spread out' or 'Create space' is a complete waste of time, so it's better to go with the natural instincts of the kids and try not to get frustrated.

Remember: They are having fun chasing the ball so please don't turn them off the game by telling them they are doing the wrong thing.

What you can do for these young players in training is reduce the numbers of players in the small-sided games to 3 v. 3 or 4 v. 4 so that there are less players crowding around the ball and the kids get more chance of a kick.

Having said that, young players eventually have to learn to find space so that they can receive a pass from their team-mates, otherwise they will become frustrated and their enjoyment of the game will diminish.

Learning to create space for receiving a pass will be developed through playing the

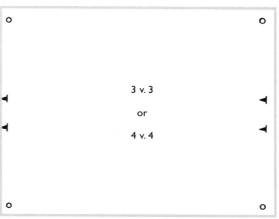

3 v. 3

or

4 v. 4

Very young players can play 3 v. 3 or 4 v. 4 in training

full game and small-sided games, but there are also certain exercises that you can use to shortcut the learning process.

Before outlining these exercises it is important that you have a basic understanding of exactly what is meant by creating space.

WHAT DO WE MEAN BY 'CREATING SPACE'?

Space is a combination of distance and angle.
Distance: The actual number of metres the player is away from the nearest defender when he receives the ball.

The *greater* this distance, the more *time* the player will have to control the ball, get his head up and make a decision because the defender has further to run to make a challenge. Your player will be, and look, a better player just by doing this—as the following examples indicate:

In Diagram 1, Player B has positioned himself to receive a pass from Player A, but Player B is only 4 m from the nearest defender (Player C). Once the ball is passed by Player A, Player C has to move only a few metres to put Player B under pressure. Player B has *less than 4 m of time* to control the ball, get his head up, make a decision as to what to do with the ball and actually do it! He has positioned himself far too close to the nearest defender.

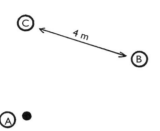

Diagram 1: Player B is far too close to the nearest defender and has little time (only 4 m) to perform the skills of the game when he receives the ball.

The situation in Diagram 2 is much better. Player B has positioned himself 12 m from the nearest defender (Player C), who has to run *three times as far* to pressure Player B. Player B now has three times the amount of time to control the ball, look up, make a decision and do something constructive with the ball.

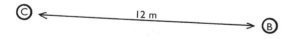

Diagram 2: Player B has increased the time he can perform on the ball by moving further away from the nearest defender

Summary
The **less distance** the receiving attacker who is about to receive the ball is away from the nearest defender, the **less time** he will have to perform the skills of the game.

The **greater distance** the receiving attacker who is about to receive the ball is from the nearest defender the **more time** he will have to perform the skills of the game.

Angle: The other key factor in creating space and being in a good position to receive a pass is to position your attacking players at the correct angle of support to the player with the ball.

It may sound simplistic, but those attacking players not in possession of the ball must position themselves so that the player with the ball can *see them* and have a *clear path to pass to them*. See the following examples:

In Diagram 3, Player A cannot pass to Player B because Player B is hidden behind the defender, Player C. However in Diagram 4 Player B has changed his angle of support so Player A can see him and pass to him.

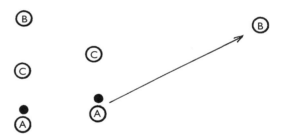

LEFT Diagram 3: Player A cannot pass to Player B because Player B is not at the correct angle
RIGHT: Diagram 4: Player A can now make the pass as Player B is at a good angle to receive the ball

Effective passing is the cornerstone of the game of soccer and being at the correct distance and angle to receive a pass from the player with the ball is in turn one of the keys to effective passing.

Too often coaches and spectators blame the player with the ball for making a bad pass or losing possession of the ball, when the fault is in fact with the team-mates who are in poor positions to receive the ball.

EXERCISES TO CREATE SPACE

Exercise 1: 3 Attackers v. 1 Defender

Objective: To teach players how to create space by supporting the player with the ball at the correct distance and angle.

EXERCISE SET-UP:

- Mark out the required number of grids, dimensions 10 m × 10 m.
- Have three attackers playing against one defender in each grid (see Diagram 5).

EXERCISE RULES:

- The attackers have to keep the ball away from the defender for as long as possible.
- The defender must always challenge the person with the ball.
- If the defender wins the ball, he must pass it back to one of the attackers and the exercise recommences.
- This exercise can be scored by counting the number of consecutive passes made by the three attackers.
- The coach should change the defender with one of the attackers approximately every minute.

COACHING RULES:

Introduce the following three key rules progressively and in the following order:

Diagram 5: Players run only along the lines

Rule 1: The three attacking players must only move along the imaginary lines on the outside of the grid; this will ensure they stay out of the middle of the grid (see Diagram 5).

Rule 2: The three attacking players must get to the corners of the grid to receive the ball (while only running along the lines); see Diagram 6.

Diagram 6: Players have to get to the corners

Rule 3: All passes must be directed to the corners of the grid (while the players are still running along the lines and getting to the corners); see Diagram 7, page 98.

- Tell the players to move quickly to get into position and remain calm when receiving and passing the ball.
- This is also an excellent exercise for improving short distance passing skills.
- It is important to be patient and introduce the three coaching rules gradually. For example you may introduce the first rule in the first two training sessions, the second rule in the next two sessions, and so on.

Age Range: Nine years and upwards.

Note: You don't have to possess coaching

knowledge to use this exercise effectively. Three attackers v. 1 defender is a very simple activity if you follow the three key rules and persist with the exercise for many training sessions during the season.

Diagram 7: Players pass only to the corners

Diagrams 8 and 9 illustrate what 3 attackers v. 1 defender would probably look like before you introduce the coaching rules.

Diagram 8: The attacking players are far too close to the defender and will have little time to do anything constructive when they receive the ball

Players at the Incorrect Distance: The attacking players are so close together that one defender can do a good job against all three attackers—he only has to take a couple of steps in any direction to put the player receiving the ball under pressure (see Diagram 8).

Players at the Wrong Angle: As well as the attacking players being too close to each other, one of the attacking players (Player A3) is 'hiding' behind the defender and is in the wrong position to receive a pass from Player A1.

This makes the defender's job very easy as he is effectively playing against only two attackers (see Diagram 9).

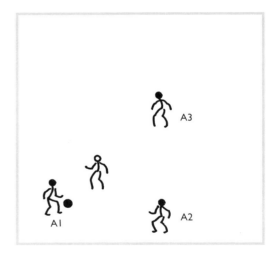

Diagram 9: The players are far too close to the defender and Player A3 is at the wrong angle to receive the ball.

Once you have introduced the three key rules the players will, over a period of time begin to resemble a perfect picture of players creating space (see Diagram 10, page 99).

By achieving the correct angle and distance (i.e. receiving the ball in the corners), the attacking players will start to look like better players because:

■ when the players are in possession of the ball they have two people to whom they may pass.

- when they receive the ball they have *more time* to perform because the defender has further to run to put pressure on them.

Diagram 10: Players are at the correct distance and angle

If your players are having trouble with the above exercise, mark out a grid 20 m × 20 m and let the kids play 4 attackers v. 1 defender or 5 attackers v. 1 defender, with no coaching rules as an introductory exercise.
Note: This is only to get the players used to the idea of creating space; it is not a game-like exercise.

Exercise 2: 4 Attackers v. 2 Defenders

Objective: This is the next progression from 3 attackers v. 1 defender. This exercise takes players to the next level of creating space and supporting the player on the ball at the correct distance and angle. It is also an excellent exercise for improving short range passing.

EXERCISE SET-UP:

- Mark out a series of grids 20 m × 20 m (see Diagram 11, page 100).
- Have four attackers playing against two defenders in each grid.
- The two defenders should wear coloured bibs to distinguish them from the attackers.

EXERCISE RULES:

- The four attackers have to keep the ball away from the two defenders for as long as possible; one of the two defenders must challenge the person on the ball.
- If the defenders win the ball they must pass it back to an attacker and the exercise recommences.
- This exercise can be scored by counting the number of consecutive passes made by the four attackers.
- The coach should change two of the defenders and two of the attackers approximately every minute.

COACHING RULES:

Introduce the following three key rules progressively and in the following order:

Rule 1: Attacking players must only receive the ball along the imaginary lines on the outside of the grid (see Diagram 11, page 100).

Rule 2: Place a marker at the midpoint on each grid line. Each of the four attackers must get to either the markers or the corners of the grid to receive the ball, but are not allowed to go past their midpoint markers. This rule effectively divides the large grid into four smaller individual grids and stops players crowding (see Diagram 12, page 100).

Rule 3: The player with the ball should pass to either the corner of the grid or the markers at the midpoint of the grid (see Diagram 13, page 100).
Age Range: Nine/10 years and upwards—depending on the skill level of your players and how well they have succeeded at Exercise 1.
Note: Four attackers v. 2 defenders is a simple yet excellent exercise in which the coach doesn't have to actually coach; instead just follow the three key rules.

Before you introduce the three key rules, Exercise 2 will probably look a lot like Diagram 14 on page 101. Once you have

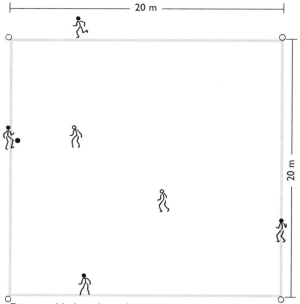

Diagram 11.:Attacking players move along the lines only

the progression from Exercise 1 to Exercise 2, then by all means let them play 5 attackers v. 2 defenders in a 20 m × 20 m area with no coaching rules until they are more confident with the exercise and more competent at supporting the player on the ball at the correct distance and angle.

Exercise 3: 6 Attackers v. 3 Defenders

Objective: To take players to the next level of creating space by supporting the player on the ball at the correct distance and angle in a very realistic and game-like situation. This exercise will also improve short passing, long passing and player awareness.

EXERCISE SET-UP:
- Mark out an area approximately the size of a quarter of the full-size pitch.
- The three defenders should wear coloured bibs to distinguish them from the six attackers.

EXERCISE RULES:
- The six attacking players have to keep the ball away from the three defending players for as long as possible. One of the defend-

introduced the coaching rules the players will, over a period of time, start to resemble Diagram 15 on page 101; i.e. the attacking players will be making themselves available to receive a pass at the correct angle and distance. *Note*: If your players are having trouble with

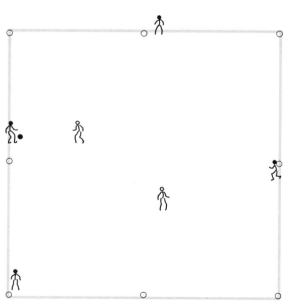

Diagram 12:Attacking players are not allowed past the midpoint markers

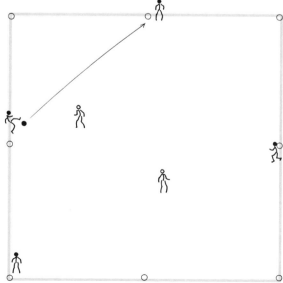

Diagram 13: Players can only pass to the midpoint markers or the corners of the grid

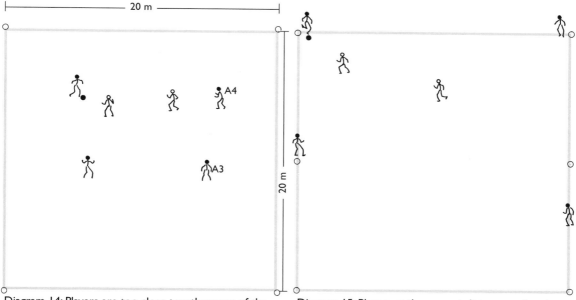

Diagram 14: Players are too close together; one of the major faults will be poor supporting angles as is the case with Player A3 and Player A4

Diagram 15: Players at the correct distance and angle are in excellent positions to receive the ball

ing players must challenge the player on the ball.

- If the defenders win the ball they must pass it back to an attacker and the exercise recommences.
- This exercise can be scored by counting the number of consecutive passes. A certain number of passes can equate to a goal (e.g. in the case of younger players, four consecutive passes could equal a goal). As your players become more competent at this exercise the number of passes required for a goal can increase.
- The coach should change the defenders around approximately every two to three minutes.

COACHING RULES:

The main problem you will face with this exercise is that the six attackers will finish up in one half of the playing area crowding around the ball. There are two key rules you can introduce to avoid this:

Rule 1: Place markers at the four midpoints of the playing area as shown in Diagram 16 on page 102.

These markers divide the playing area into quarters. Start the exercise by placing one attacker in each quarter of the playing area, with the instructions that they must stay within that quarter area. The other two attackers are free to move anywhere they want. This rule will reduce crowding around the ball. *Note*: If you find that your players still crowd too much, insist that the four players allocated to their quarter areas receive the ball on the imaginary lines on the outside of the grid.

Rule 2: This is a very simple progression of the first rule. Of the six attacking players, the coach restricts two players to one half of the playing area, another two players to the other half of the playing area, with the remaining two players free to move anywhere they like.

Again, this rule reduces crowding around the ball (see Diagram 17, page 102).

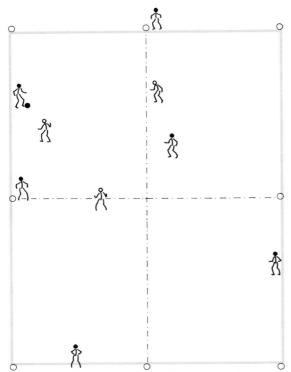

Diagram 16: Four of the six attackers are restricted to their own quarter of the pitch

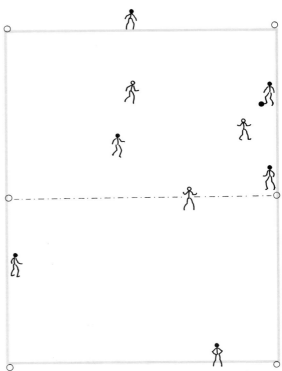

Diagram 17: Space is created by restricting two players to their half of the area

Note: As well as changing the defenders around, the coach should also give every player a turn as one of the two free-roaming attackers.

Age Range: Once players are fairly competent at the 4 attackers v. 2 defenders exercise, this exercise can be introduced. It is probably best suited to players aged around 10/11 years and up.

Before you introduce the above rules, Exercise 3 will probably look like Diagram 18 on page 103.

Once you have introduced the two key rules the attacking players will, over a period of time, start to use the full playing area (i.e. the full amount of space available); see Diagram 19, page 103.

With all of the above exercises (3 v. 1, 4 v. 2, 6 v. 3), you can remove the coaching rules once the players have got the idea of creating

space. You may find that after you remove the rules the players go back to their old habits. If this is the case, re-introduce the rules for a spell and then remove them again; keep doing this until the players can perform well without the rules.

OTHER METHODS FOR CREATING SPACE

Exercise 4: 3 attackers v. No defenders

Objective: To teach players to spread out when in possession of the ball.

EXERCISE SET-UP:

Use markers to divide the pitch vertically into thirds from the penalty area to the halfway line (see Diagram 20, page 103).

EXERCISE RULES:

- Players are to progress down the field, but only staying in their third of the pitch.
- Any player can finish with a shot at goal.

Diagram 18: The six players will finish up in one half of the playing area crowding around the ball

Diagram 19: Because of the key rules, players are using the full amount of space available

Age Range: Eight/nine years and upwards.

Once your players have become proficient at the above exercise, you can introduce the following variations:

(i) 3 attackers v. 1 defender: Set up the exercise exactly as above—but introduce a defender. The defender is free to challenge for the ball in any third of the pitch (see Diagram 21, page 104).

(ii) 4 attackers v. 2 defenders: Set up this exercise exactly as above, except there are four attackers and two defenders, with two attackers in the middle third (see Diagram 22, page 104).

For older players, introduce more attackers and defenders; for example, 5 attackers v. 3 defenders, 4 attackers v. 3 defenders, 6 attackers v. 3 defenders, etc.

Remember—the more defensive players you introduce, the more difficult the exercise becomes.

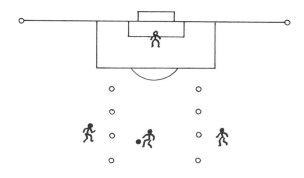

Diagram 20: 3 attackers v. 0 defenders

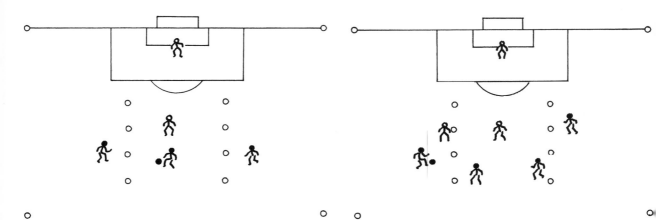

Diagram 21: 3 attackers v. 1 defender

Diagram 22: 4 attackers v. 2 defenders

VARIOUS SMALL-SIDED GAMES FOR CREATING SPACE
Exercise 5: Four Goal Game
Objective: This game encourages the attacking players to spread out, create space and switch the direction of play. It is also an excellent exercise for developing player awareness.

EXERCISE SET-UP:
- Pitch size depends on the number of players. For a 5-a-side a quarter of a full-size pitch would be about right.
- Players should be wearing coloured bibs.
- Set up two 3 m goals at each end of the pitch (see Diagram 23A).
- If you have any young players who have

Diagram 23A: The four goal game, players can score in two goals

Diagram 23B: With two full-size goals, this is also a good game for goalkeepers

decided they want to be specialist goalkeepers then you can make one or more of the 3 m goals a full-size 8 yard goal (see the set-up in Diagram 23B, page 104) so they can also practise.

EXERCISE RULES:

Each team has two goals to score through and two goals to defend.

COACHING POINTS:

The coach should encourage the player on the ball to get his head up and look to switch play. *Age Range*: Open—this game is worth trying at any age.

Exercise 6: Six Goal Game

Objective: This game is an extension of the four goal game and encourages attacking players to spread out, use the width of the field and switch the direction of play. It is also an excellent exercise for developing player awareness.

EXERCISE SET-UP:

■ Set up with two goals at each end of the pitch and one 3 m goal at the midpoint of each touchline (see Diagram 24).
■ Pitch size depends on the number of players. For 5-a-side a quarter of a full-size pitch would be about right.
■ Players should wear coloured bibs.

EXERCISE RULES:

■ Each team attacks two end goals and both side goals (see Diagram 25).
■ Players score through the side goals by passing through the goal to another player on the same team; once they have scored in this way they keep possession and the game continues.

COACHING POINTS:

The coach should encourage the player in possession of the ball to get his head up and look to switch play. *Age Range*: 10/11 years and upwards.

Exercise 7: No Goals, Keep Possession

Objective: Encourages the team in possession of the ball to use the full area of the pitch; it also encourages attacking players to support the player on the ball.

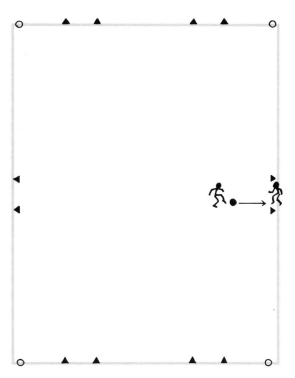

Diagram 24: Six goal game (note the players are scoring a goal by passing through a side goal)

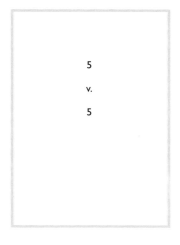

Diagram 25: No goals, keep possession

EXERCISE SET-UP:

- For 5-a-side play in a quarter of a full size pitch (see Diagram 25, page 105).
- There are no goals.

EXERCISE RULES:

Players score points by keeping possession of the ball for a certain number of passes.

Note: Choose a number of passes that is achievable and gradually increase this number as the players become more competent—for example, for 10-year-olds, the initial number of passes may be as low as four.

Age Range: 10/11 years and upwards.

SECTION III
Putting it All Together

So far this book has provided you with information on how to get the best out of young players, along with a substantial number of exercises to help the children develop their soccer skills.

This section focuses on how to apply this previous information to different age groups effectively. It is very important that training sessions take the significant differences between age groups into account. A seven-year-old and a 10-year-old are light years apart in physical development, attention span and understanding of concepts such as teamwork, etc. The next two chapters will enable you to tailor your training sessions to suit the age group you are coaching.

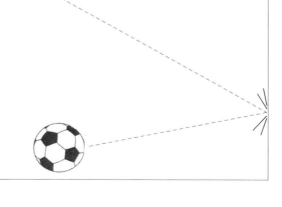

Coaching Different Age Groups

Training sessions must vary in content and length, according to the different age groups. The following are sample training sessions for different age groups. Naturally, these training sessions should ensure lots of repetition, fun and enjoyment, praise/positive feedback and small-sided games.

Before we detail the sample training sessions, it's important to look at two issues that seem to be a source of confusion amongst coaches of young players—warm ups and fitness.

Warm ups: Generally speaking, stretches and warm ups are not necessary prior to the age of 10 (some kids don't even need a warm up at age 10). If you think about it, little seven-year-old Johnny doesn't do stretches in the kitchen before he sprints across the street to play with his mate!

So don't waste your time on warm ups and stretches for six- to nine-year-olds. In fact, you will see in the sample training sessions to follow that the training sessions for this age group start with a small-sided game to get the kids straight into it.
Note: Some boys at around age nine will mature early and may develop muscle mass in the legs. They may need to be taught how to perform a stretching routine.

Fitness: Until the age of approximately 14/15 years, a properly constructed training session will mean there is no need for fitness work without a ball. The average club player should be able to get all the fitness they need from small-sided games and exercises.

Naturally, if a player wants to undertake fitness work in their own time then this should be encouraged.
Note: The small-sided game 3 v. 3 is a great fitness builder and can be used as such for players from 11/12 years of age and up.

TRAINING SESSIONS FOR SIX- AND SEVEN-YEAR-OLDS
These children have a very short attention span so you can't do any skill exercises for more than 5 minutes at a time. In fact, all they want to do is run around and kick the ball and this means lots of small-sided games.

Out of a 1 hour session, about 45–50 minutes should be spent on small-sided games and to ensure they get lots of touches of the ball these games should be 3-a-side or 4-a-side. Obviously the size of your small-sided games will depend on the number of kids at training.
Note: Remember to let them play at their own pace in the small-sided games.

Sample 1 Hour Session (Six/Seven Years)
Start session

0–15 minutes: Small-sided games (no warm up needed)

15–20 minutes: Awareness exercise in a grid

20–30 minutes: Small-sided games

30–35 minutes: Skill development exercise (i.e. choose a skill to practise such as heading, passing, shooting, etc.).

35–45 minutes: Small-sided games

45–50 minutes: Skill development exercise (i.e. choose a skill to practise such as heading, passing, shooting, etc.)

50–60 minutes: Small-sided games
Finish session

Note: For six- and seven-year-olds, fun and enjoyment are the number one priority.

TRAINING SESSIONS FOR EIGHT-YEAR-OLDS

These sessions are very similar to those for six- and seven-year-olds; the main difference is that the skill exercises can be slightly longer than 5 minutes (i.e. 5–10 minutes).

Out of a 1 hour session, approximately 40 minutes should be allocated to small-sided games and 20 minutes to skill exercises. The small-sided games can vary between 3-a-side and 5-a-side. Obviously, the size of your small-sided games will be determined by the number of kids who are at training.

Sample 1 Hour Session (Eight Years)
Start session
0–10 minutes: Small-sided games (no warm ups needed)
10–15 minutes: Awareness exercise in a grid
15–25 minutes: Small-sided games
25–35 minutes: Skill development exercise (i.e. choose a skill to practise such as heading, passing, shooting, etc.)
35–45 minutes: Small-sided games
45–55 minutes: Skill development exercise (i.e. choose a skill to practise such as heading, passing, shooting, etc.).
55–65 minutes: Small-sided games
Finish session

Note: Fun and enjoyment are still the number one priority, but there is an increased focus on skill development.

TRAINING SESSIONS FOR NINE-YEAR-OLDS

It seems that at around nine years of age, children move into a new level of maturity and understanding as far as learning soccer (or any other sport) is concerned. There is therefore the opportunity to perform a wider range of skill exercises and for slightly longer periods of time. Training sessions can now be extended to approximately 1¼ hours.

Out of a 1¼ hour session, about 45–50 minutes should be allocated to small-sided games and 25–30 minutes to skill exercises. The small-sided games can vary from 3-a-side to 6-a-side. Obviously, the size of your small-sided games will be determined by the number of kids at training. From this age upwards, repetition of a skill is increasingly accepted by the kids as necessary to improve skill levels.

Sample 1¼ Hour Session (Nine Years)
Start session
0–10 minutes: Small-sided games (no warm ups needed)
10–20 minutes: Passing practice
20–30 minutes: Small-sided games
30–40 minutes: Group skill development exercise (e.g. 3 attackers v. 1 defender)
45–50 minutes: Small-sided games (could be a multi-goal game)
50–65 minutes: Awareness exercise (5 minutes)
Heading or shooting exercise (10 minutes)
65–75 minutes: Small-sided games
Finish session

Note: Fun and enjoyment are still a priority, but you will now aim to provide that through increased skill development.

TRAINING SESSIONS FOR 10- AND 11-YEAR-OLDS

Training sessions for 10- and 11-year-olds should last approximately 1½ hours and include a warm up and stretches.

Out of a 1½ hour session, approximately 10 minutes should be spent on the warm up (including stretches), 40 minutes on skill exercises and 40 minutes on small-sided games. This age group is starting to understand the need to work together as a team, so skill exercises can start to include more gridwork such as 3 v. 1, 4 v. 2, and 6 v. 3. The small-sided games can vary from 3-a-side to 6-a-side and can include small-sided games such as multi-goal games. Obviously the size of your small-sided games will be determined by the number of kids at training.

Sample 1½ Hour Session (10/11 Years)

Start session

0–10 minutes: Warm up and stretches (see Appendix II for details on stretching exercises).

10–25 minutes: Small-sided games

25–40 minutes: Creating space (e.g. gridwork 3 v. 1, 4 v. 2, 6 v. 3)

40–55 minutes: Creating space (small-sided multi-goal game)

55–80 minutes: Shooting exercise (15 minutes)

Heading practice (10 minutes)

80–90 minutes: Small-sided games

90–95 minutes: Stretches to finish

Finish session

THE SUCCESSFUL TRAINING SESSION

For all successful training sessions, remember the following rules:

Rule 1: Prepare Training Sessions on Paper

Rule 2: Quick Organisation

Rule 3: Positive and Purposeful

Rule 4: Enthusiasm

Rule 5: Look and Act the Part

Rule 6: Correct Equipment

Combine the above rules with those below, which also should be present in every training session.

1. *Repetition*—Players must have an enormous amount of ball contact in every training session.

2. *Fun and Enjoyment*—Players must enjoy themselves

3. *Praise and Positive Reinforcement*—Catch players doing something right; praise progress.

4. *Small-Sided Games*—Make sure a substantial part of any training session consists of small-sided games.

5. *Coaching*—One ounce of coaching to one ton of practice.

6. *Demonstration*—A picture is worth a thousand words. Don't talk about what you want, show them instead; if you can't demonstrate it yourself then have a player demonstrate for you.

Remember: Coaching and demonstration are preferable, but not essential for a productive and effective training session.

In all your training sessions:

- Use every minute of the training session.
- Don't have players standing around doing nothing or stood in queues waiting their turn.
- Avoid wasting time talking to the boys about the game; for players aged upwards of 10/11 years, it's okay to talk about last week's or this week's game whilst the players are stretching. Ask them how they think they performed as a team and where they think there is room for improvement.
- Keep all the players involved.
- Keep the players active.

Note: in between exercises players can practice individual ball juggling or keeping the ball in the air between two, depending on their level of ability.

Allow brief and regular rest periods for players to have a drink, especially in hot and humid conditions.

The majority of coaches involved with junior soccer are unpaid and working in a full-time job at least five days a week. It is so easy to fall into the trap of just turning up for training unprepared and with little drive and enthusiasm after a hard day's work. I can only say that if you approach training with the above points in mind then you will energise the kids and energise yourself, thereby achieving real satisfaction in a job well done. **The more you put in, the more you will get out.**

Appendices

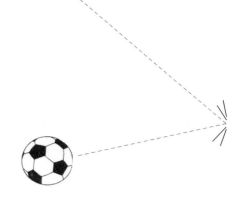

APPENDIX I: THROW INS

The Laws of the Game (see Appendix IV, page 115) state that at the moment the thrower delivers the ball into play he must be facing the field of play and part of each foot should be either on the touch line or on the ground behind the touch line.

The main problem for young players is that they lift one or both feet off the ground, which is a foul throw.

The other Law of the Game that young players have a problem with is, 'the thrower shall use both hands and shall deliver the ball from behind and over his head'.

Put another way, this means that the player must ensure the throw is *one continuous motion* from behind the head. This is a problem with children who have a tendency to stop their arms halfway through the throwing motion and start again.

When a player breaks the Laws of the Game which apply to throw ins, the referee rules that a foul throw has occurred and awards the throw to the opposition from the same spot on the touch line.

Incorrect: the player has lifted his foot off the ground

Correct: both feet are in contact with the ground

APPENDIX II:
WARM UPS AND STRETCHING

Warm ups and stretches are not essential for most children prior to 10 years of age.* From 10 years and up it is necessary to commence training sessions with a 10-minute warm up and stretching routine to reduce the chance of injury.

It is important that players get a slight sweat through exercises or running prior to performing stretches, so that they aren't stretching cold muscles. This running should preferably involve a ball but avoid any sharp movements such as shooting. Dribbling and passing exercises are ideal.

Some basic rules for stretching are:

- Stretch gently and slowly until there is a feeling of tension and discomfort in the muscle being stretched. Never bounce into the stretching position or stretch in a violent manner.
- The key muscles to stretch for soccer are the calf, hamstring, groin and thigh muscles.
- Have the players stretch for 5 minutes at the end of each training session. The muscles are very warm and the players will be able to stretch further and develop greater flexibility.
- Breathe normally when stretching.
- Each stretch should be held for 10–15 seconds.

Stretching Exercises

The following stretches are the most important for soccer players and should be performed three times with each leg and held for 10–15 seconds.

- Calf:
  The back and front feet face the same way as the body.
  Keep the back leg straight and push the

heel to the floor.
Hold for 10 seconds.
This exercise can done against a fence or with a partner.

- Hamstring:
  Bend from the hips, slowly sliding the hands down the leg; try to touch the toes.
  Hold for 10 seconds.

- Groin:
  Press the arms outward and the legs inward.
  Hold for 10 seconds.

*Some nine-year-old children can mature early; they can be quite bulky in muscle build. If this is the case a brief warm up may well be necessary for these players.

- Thigh:
  Pull the leg up by the ankle.
  Lean slightly forward from the hip.
  Hold for 10 seconds.
  This exercise can be performed against a fence or with a partner.

Fitness and Weight Training

Fitness: Specific fitness sessions without a ball (such as sprints and endurance runs) are not generally necessary before the age of fifteen years. A properly constructed training session where the players are active and involved will provide all the fitness a young player requires and at the same time develop their soccer ability. Small-sided games such as 3 v. 3 are excellent for developing both fitness and playing ability.

Weight Training: There is every chance of serious injury if children undertake weight training at too young an age. This definitely applies to pre-adolescent and young adolescent children. **Weight training for any young player should only be commenced with the approval and strict guidance of a highly qualified supervisor.**

APPENDIX III:
DEALING WITH INJURIES

This section is concerned with the immediate management of non-severe injuries. It in no way gives you the knowledge to deal with serious injuries (such as broken bones, spinal injuries, etc.). Serious injuries should be dealt with by qualified personnel.

Injury Prevention: Some Basic Pointers
- For children aged 10 years and over, warm ups and stretches should be undertaken prior to training and games.
- Players should wear shin pads at training as well as during the game.
- In hot and/or humid conditions players should consume the equivalent of one glass of water every 15 minutes. This is most important as **heat exhaustion is a very serious problem and children are particularly susceptible.** Keep in mind that thirst is the last indicator of the need for fluid intake.
- Players should wear sunscreen as required.
- Players should not undertake physical activity when ill.
- Players should not return to playing too soon after sustaining an injury.
- Sprinkler heads should be covered with a soft marker.

Severe Injury
For potentially serious injuries such as spinal injury or broken bones, summon professional help immediately. Err on the side of caution and **do not** move the player.

Less Severe Injury
This is where the RICED process can dramatically reduce the time an injured player spends away from the game. The RICED regime is used for bumps, bruises, corks, muscle and ligament injuries, sprains and strains.
RICED stands for:
Rest the injured area;
Ice the injured area for 15–20 minutes every 2 hours for the first 48 hours. The ice will reduce the swelling;
Note: Do not apply ice directly to the skin as this can cause ice burns.
Compression: A firm wide bandage should be applied over the injury and the area surrounding the injury. Compression will reduce the swelling;
Elevation: If possible, raise the injured area above the level of the heart as this will reduce blood flow to the area and reduce swelling;
Diagnosis: Have the player visit a sports injury professional as soon as possible.

The RICED procedure is a simple and effective method for immediate management of non-severe injuries.

APPENDIX IV:
LAWS OF THE GAME

The following are the most important and most commonly used rules in the game of soccer. For complete details of the rules of the game, *The Official Laws of the Game Handbook* can be purchased from your State Soccer Federation (see page 118 for details).

Throw In

A throw in is a method of restarting play. A goal cannot be scored directly from a throw in.

A throw in is awarded:
(i)   when the whole of the ball passes over the touch line, either on the ground or in the air;
(ii) from the point where it crossed the touch line;
(iii) to the opponents of the player who last touched the ball.

PROCEDURE

At the moment of delivering the ball, the thrower:
(i)   faces the field of play;
(ii) has part of each foot either on the touch line or on the ground outside the touch line;
(iii) uses both hands;
(iv) delivers the ball from behind and over his head.

The thrower may not touch the ball until it has touched or been touched by another player.

The ball is in play immediately it enters the field of play.

Ball Out of Play

The ball is out of play when:
(i)   it has wholly crossed the goal line or touch line, whether on the ground or in the air;
(ii) the game has been stopped by the referee.

Offside

OFFSIDE POSITION

It is not an offence in itself to be in an offside position.

A player is in an offside position if he is nearer to his opponents' goal line than both the ball and the second last opponent.

A player is not in an offside position if:
(i)   he is in his own half of the field of play;
or
(ii) he is level with the second last opponent;
or
(iii) he is level with the last two opponents.

OFFENCE

A player in an offside position is only penalised if, at the moment the ball touches or is played by one of his team, he is, in the opinion of the referee, involved in active play by:
(i)   interfering with play;
or
(ii) interfering with an opponent;
or
(iii) gaining an advantage by being in that position.

NO OFFENCE

There is no offside offence if a player receives the ball directly from:
(i)   a goal kick;
or
(ii) a throw-in;
or
(iii) a corner kick.

INFRINGEMENT/SANCTIONS

For any offside offence, the referee awards an indirect free kick to the opposing team to be taken from the place where the infringement occurred.

Free Kicks

TYPES OF FREE KICKS

Free kicks are either direct or indirect.
For both direct and indirect free kicks, the ball must be stationary when the kick is taken and the kicker does not touch the ball a second time until it has touched another player.

THE DIRECT FREE KICK

(i)   if a direct free kick is kicked directly into the opponents' goal, a goal is awarded;

(ii) if a direct free kick is kicked directly into the team's own goal, a corner kick is awarded to the opposing team.

The Indirect Free Kick

SIGNAL

The referee indicates an indirect free kick by raising his arm above his head. He maintains his arm in that position until the kick has been taken and the ball has touched another player or goes out of play.

BALL ENTERS THE GOAL

A goal can be scored only if the ball subsequently touches another player before it enters the goal.

(i)   if an indirect free kick is kicked directly into the opponents' goal, a goal kick is awarded;

(ii) if an indirect free kick is kicked directly into the team's own goal, a corner kick is awarded to the opposing team.

Position of Free Kick

FREE KICK INSIDE THE PENALTY AREA

Direct or indirect free kick to the defending team:

(i)   all opponents are at least 9.15 m (10 yds) from the ball;

(ii) all opponents remain outside the penalty area until the ball is in play;

(iii) the ball is in play when it is kicked directly beyond the penalty area;

(iv) a free kick awarded in the goal area is taken from any point inside that area.

Indirect free kick to the attacking team:

(i)   all opponents are at least 9.15 m (10 yds) from the ball until it is in play, unless they are on their own goal line between the goalposts;

(ii) the ball is in play when it is kicked and moves;

(iii) an indirect free kick awarded inside the goal area is taken from that part of the goal area line which runs parallel to the goal line, at the point nearest to where the infringement occurred.

FREE KICK OUTSIDE THE PENALTY AREA

(i)   all opponents are at least 9.15 m (10 yds) from the ball until it is in play;

(ii) the ball is in play when it is kicked and moves;

(iii) the free kick is taken from the place where the infringement occurred.

Fouls and Misconduct

Fouls result in either a direct free kick or an indirect free kick; the difference between the two is as follows:

- *Direct Free Kick*: the player can score directly from the free kick.
- *Indirect Free Kick*: these kicks must touch another player (on either team), before a goal can be scored.

DIRECT FREE KICK

A direct free kick is awarded to the opposing team if a player commits any of the following six offences in a manner considered by the referee to be careless, reckless or involving excessive force:

(i)   kicks or attempts to kick an opponent;

(ii) trips or attempts to trip an opponent;

(iii) jumps at an opponent;

(iv) charges an opponent;

(v)   strikes or attempts to strike an opponent;

(vi) pushes an opponent.

A direct free kick is also to be awarded to the opposing team if a player commits any of the following four offences:

(i)   tackles an opponent to gain possession of the ball, making contact with the opponent before touching the ball;

(ii) holds an opponent;

(iii) spits at an opponent;

(iv) handles the ball deliberately (except for the goalkeeper within his penalty area).

A direct free kick is taken from where the offence occurred.

PENALTY KICK

A penalty kick is awarded if any of the above ten offences is committed by a player inside his own penalty area, irrespective of the position of the ball, provided it is in play.

INDIRECT FREE KICK

An indirect free kick is awarded to the opposing team if a player, in the opinion of the referee, commits any of the following offences:

(i)   plays in a dangerous manner;
(ii)   impedes the progress of an opponent;
(iii) prevents the goalkeeper from releasing the ball from his hands.

An indirect free kick is also awarded to the opposing team if a goalkeeper, inside his own penalty area, commits any of the following offences:

(i)   takes more than four steps while controlling the ball with his hands, before releasing it from his possession;
(ii)   touches the ball again with his hands after it has been released from his possession and has not touched any other player;
(iii) touches the ball with his hands after it has been deliberately kicked to him by a team-mate;
(iv)   wastes time.

The indirect free kick is taken from where the offence occurred.

The above are taken from Laws of The Game 1997,
Published by Fédération Internationale de Football Association,
11 Hitzigweg, 8030 Zurich, Switzerland

Disciplinary Sanctions

CAUTIONABLE OFFENCES

A player is cautioned and shown the yellow card if he commits any of the following seven offences:

1. Is guilty of unsporting behaviour.
2. Shows dissent by word or action.
3. Persistently infringes the Laws of the Game.
4. Delays the restart of play.
5. Fails to respect the required distance when play is restarted with a corner kick or free kick.
6. Enters or re-enters the field of play without the referee's permission.
7. Deliberately leaves the field of play without the referee's permission.

SENDING-OFF OFFENCES

A player is sent off and shown the red card if he commits any of the following seven offences:

1. Is guilty of serious foul play.
2. Is guilty of violent conduct.
3. Spits at an opponent or any other person.
4. Denies an opponent a goal or an obvious goal-scoring opportunity by deliberately handling the ball (this does not apply to a goalkeeper within his own penalty area).
5. Denies an obvious goal-scoring opportunity to an opponent moving towards the player's goal by an offence punishable by a free kick or a penalty kick.
6. Uses offensive, insulting or abusive language.
7. Receives a second caution in the same match.

APPENDIX V:
GETTING HELP—SOCCER
FEDERATIONS

For details on the various coaching courses available contact your nearest Soccer Federation:

NATIONAL BODY
Soccer Australia
PO Box 175, Paddington NSW 2021
Ph: (02) 9380 6099
Fax: (02) 9380 6155

STATE BODIES
Australian Capital Territory
Soccer Canberra
PO Box 405, Canberra ACT 2601
Ph: (02) 6260 4000
Fax: (02) 6260 4999

New South Wales:
Soccer NSW
235–257 Meurants Lane
Glenwood NSW 2768
Ph: (02) 9629 1800
Fax: (02) 9629 3770

Northern New South Wales:
NNSW Soccer Federation
235 Old Maitland Road
Hexham NSW 2322
Ph: (02) 4964 8922
Fax: (02) 4964 8921

Northern Territory:
Northern Territory Soccer Federation
GPO Box 3105, Darwin NT 0801
Ph: (08) 8981 4477
Fax: (08) 8981 3313

Queensland:
Queensland Soccer Federation
Perry Park
Abbotsford Road
Mayne QLD 4006
Ph: (07) 3252 5327
Fax: (07) 3252 1137

South Australia:
South Australia Soccer Federation
PO Box 110, Hindmarsh SA 5007
Ph: (08) 8340 0688
Fax: (08) 8340 1570

Tasmania:
Soccer Tasmania
PO Box 371, Glenorchy TAS 7010
Ph: (03) 6272 9748
Fax: (03) 6272 8868

Victoria:
Victorian Soccer Federation
23 Dorcas Street
South Melborne VIC 3205
Ph: (03) 9682 9666
Fax: (03) 9682 9777

Western Australia:
Soccer Administration of Western Australia
PO Box 188, Jolimont WA 6014
Ph: (08) 9383 7878
Fax: (08) 9383 7883

Index

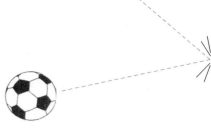